THE BATTLE AGAINST INTERVENTION, 1939–1941

By
Justus D. Doenecke

AN ANVIL ORIGINAL
under the general editorship of
Hans L. Trefousse

KRIEGER PUBLISHING COMPANY
MALABAR, FLORIDA
1997

Excerpt from *The Wave of the Future*, copyright 1940 and renewed 1968 by
Anne Morrow Lindbergh, reprinted by permission of Harcourt Brace & Company.

Original Edition   1997

Printed and Published by
KRIEGER PUBLISHING COMPANY
KRIEGER DRIVE
MALABAR, FLORIDA 32950

Copyright © 1997 by Justus D. Doenecke

Library of Congress Cataloging-in-Publication Data

Doenecke, Justus D.
     The battle against intervention, 1939–1941 / by Justus D.
  /Doenecke. — Original ed.
        p.   cm.
     "An Anvil original."
     "Part II: Documents" (p.) contains a collection of 34 speeches,
  articles, essays, etc.
     Includes bibliographical references (p.) and index.
ISBN 0-89464-901-9 (alk. paper)
     1. World War, 1939-1945—United States. 2. Neutrality—United
  States. 3. United States—Politics and government—1933-1945.
  I. Title.
  D769.1.D64   1997
  940.54′0973—dc20   96-18599
                                                       CIP

10 9 8 7 6 5 4 3 2

For Arthur and Norma

THE ANVIL SERIES

Anvil paperbacks give an original analysis of a major field of history or a problem area, drawing upon the most recent research. They present a concise treatment and can act as supplementary material for college history courses. Written by many of the outstanding historians in the United States, the format is one-half narrative text, one-half supporting documents, often from hard to find sources.

CONTENTS

INTRODUCTION

The Problem of Nonintervention. The years 1939–1941 marked a critical period in American history and in the world as well. At stake was nothing less than the course the United States would follow for years to come.

Most Americans remember World War II in many ways as "the good war," in which a unified nation fought against predatory and genocidal forces. It is hard to realize that the debates over the original participation of the United States were highly impassioned, manifesting an intensity only matched during the Vietnam War. On one level, the argument centered on whether the United States could subsist, indeed prosper, in a world in which Germany dominated the bulk of Europe and Japan controlled much of East Asia. On another, it focused on whether the United States could maintain its independent course, as it had for most of the past two centuries, or whether it would find its future inexorably linked to nations overseas.

To a sizable minority of the population, American security did not depend on the survival of such powers as Great Britain and China. Indeed, long after the United States entered the war, some always maintained that the foreign policy of President Franklin D. Roosevelt was at best a tragic mistake, at worst a criminal blunder. Particularly in the light of the vast expansion of Soviet power in the immediate wake of the conflict, and the later victories of communism in China and Cuba, this minority continued to argue that the United States should have remained aloof.

At the time, these people vehemently opposed Roosevelt's policies, particularly the president's efforts to aid the Allies by such measures as cash-and-carry, lend-lease, U.S. convoys to Britain, and economic sanctions upon Japan. They came from a variety of elements in American society: anti-New Deal members of Congress, Protestant and Roman Catholic leaders, midwestern industrialists, independent intellectuals, and much of the American left.

During World War II and extending into the present, these anti-interventionists often have been dismissed as "isolationists," who were at best naive obscurantists, at worst people sympathetic to the rise of ravaging totalitarian powers. True, an able scholarly literature has portrayed their real stance with much accuracy, as shown by such works as

Wayne S. Cole's *America First* (1953) and Manfred Jonas's *Isolationism in America, 1935–1941* (1966). Yet the general picture remains one of ignorant and reactionary Babbitts, living blindly in a self-created shell.

Only now are we aware of the immense diversity of American anti-interventionism. Listed in anti-interventionist ranks in 1940, for example, were a novelist who had won the Nobel Prize, one of the world's leading physiologists, possibly the nation's most respected historian, the president of the University of Chicago, experts from Columbia and Yale on international law, America's foremost architect, the head of the Congress of Industrial Organizations, and the co-founders of one of the country's most successful advertising firms. (Their names respectively: Sinclair Lewis, Anton J. Carlson, Charles A. Beard, Robert M. Hutchins, Philip Jessup, Edwin M. Borchard, Frank Lloyd Wright, John L. Lewis, Chester Bowles, and William Benton). Both John F. Kennedy and Gerald R. Ford contributed to the much-maligned America First Committee (AFC), Ford being an initial organizer of the first embryonic AFC group founded at Yale, and Kennedy listed in the AFC's large contributor's file. At the same time, the AFC's research bureau was staffed by highly educated pacifists and Socialists, who offered lengthy and cogent critiques of administration policy.

Today, the sudden end of the Cold War has left the United States groping for a coherent foreign policy. With the emergence of a new, multipolar world, Americans are continually warned against falling back into "isolationism." Ironically, however, today's debates can make an accurate picture of the old anti-interventionism more important than ever, as certain questions that these critics raised have surprising relevance today. Among their troubling queries are these: What is the potential for collective security in an era of multipower blocs? What are its limitations? What are the possible relationships between great powers and lesser ones? Can one even conceptualize a general world order, much less attempt to enforce it? Can one make general limits in defining national security? How does one define a vital interest? What is the possibility of distinguishing between *interventionism*, with its stress on unilateral action, and *internationalism*, with its emphasis on shared decision making?

A serious examination of these matters, and of how one segment of the American populace dealt with them, transcends the passion of former years. I hope this narrative and the accompanying documents will aid in an effort to grapple with issues that very much remain with us.

PART I

THE BATTLE AGAINST INTERVENTION, 1939–1941

CHAPTER 1

A THREATENED TRADITION

A Senator Delivers a Speech. Early in the afternoon of October 2, 1939, Key Pittman (Dem.-Nev.) was addressing his colleagues on the Senate floor. Rain streamed softly on the overhead skylight. Suddenly the door of the Republican cloakroom opened. Entering was a solemn-faced man of seventy-four, sporting a black suit and a black scraggly tie to match. The packed galleries had been restless, the press gallery three-fourths empty. Now the cry rang through the pressroom: "Borah's up." As the correspondents crowded in, Senator William E. Borah (Rep.-Idaho) spoke for about two hours. Toward the end of his speech, his faltering voice dropped to a whisper. When he stopped, exhausted and having less than three months to live, his political adversary Pittman walked over to shake his hand. As the galleries applauded loudly, the Senate adjourned.

Borah's speech was the opening shot in a bitter conflict between anti-interventionists and the administration of President Franklin Delano Roosevelt, one that would end only when Japanese planes sortied over Pearl Harbor. Just two weeks before Borah spoke, the president asked Congress to repeal the existing Neutrality Act, which forbade the export of American-made arms overseas. On September 1, 1939 Hitler's legions had attacked Poland, triggering British and French declarations of war against Germany two days later. Within three weeks FDR was offering Congress what was essentially a horse trade: repeal of the arms embargo and payment for all U.S. goods in cash in return for a law banning American ships from entering war zones. The proposal was called "cash-and-carry."

The address touched upon many themes that anti-interventionists would continually reiterate: that the current war was simply "another chapter in the bloody volume of European power politics," that British diplomacy had recently betrayed "the only real republic" in Eastern Europe—Czechoslovakia, and that the unspeakable battlefield horrors of less than a quarter century before were again in the offing. (*See Document No. 1.*)

To understand the points Borah raised and to see why anti-interventionism remained strong among so many Americans down to the very day of the Japanese strike, some background is necessary.

The Critical Years. In the years 1939–1941, a cataclysmic conflict broke out, far more worthy of being called a genuine world war than its predecessor, and large areas of the globe changed hands. To use the phrase of historian Gerhard L. Weinberg, the fate of the world lay "in the balance." By the end of 1941, a new German Empire dominated Western Europe and much of Eastern Europe as well. Japan appeared poised for lasting domination of all East Asia. Its empire had penetrated extensively into China, held northern Indochina, and was threatening the Philippines, Singapore, and the Netherlands East Indies. Moreover, much of France lay under direct German occupation, and its empire was divided between Vichy and Free French forces. If most of the British Empire was intact, the home isles were under siege, and such lifelines as the Suez Canal were severely menaced. The Soviet Union stood in mortal danger.

Yet, during all this time, major segments of the American public hoped that the United States would not enter this new conflict. While most sympathized with the Allied cause, they did not deem the survival of either Britain or China worth the risk of American involvement. In fact, they argued conversely—that full-scale participation in the war would help destroy whatever global balance remained and would ruin the internal fabric of American society as well.

A Matter of Definition. Both contemporaries and later historians have called the majority of these people isolationists. In his *Roosevelt and the Isolationists, 1932–45* (1983), historian Wayne S. Cole defines isolationists as those people who were "opposed to intervention in European wars" and often to conflicts in Asia and Latin America as well. They were also unilateralists, that is, they sought a "free hand" and fought collective security commitments. Because the term isolationist connotes a host of vices—indifference, dangerous naiveté, appeasement of dictators—many within its ranks preferred to be called "anti-interventionist," "noninterventionist," or "nationalist." "Americanist" was the term preferred by General Hugh Johnson, a columnist for Scripps-Howard and formerly a top New Deal administrator. Senator Arthur H. Vandenberg (Rep.-Mich.) saw himself as an "insulationist." The *New York Daily News* was one of the very few that used the name "isolationist" without apology.

A small minority of Roosevelt critics were pacifists, people who in principle opposed participation in any given conflict. Although the two camps often cooperated, isolationism could differ markedly from pacifism. One could, for example, call for strong national defense, seek overseas territories, demand economic spheres of influence, and even fight a war on one's own, and still be an isolationist; one could not engage in such activity and be a pacifist.

Of course, pacifists—like isolationists—often offered pragmatic reasons for their stance, and these reasons must be covered in any account of the antiwar movement. In the period 1939–1941, isolationists and pacifists cooperated to a surprising degree, advancing similar arguments and opposing the same legislation. If a marriage of convenience was at work, enough was held in common to call the common position "anti-interventionist."

One of the most thoughtful anti-interventionists was the historian and political scientist Charles A. Beard. A man who appeared never to be content unless he was surrounded by controversy, Beard combined an economic determinism with a strong reformist bent. In his book *A Foreign Policy for America* (1940), he advocated what he called Continental Americanism, a position whose tenets included "non-intervention in the controversies and wars of Europe and Asia." The nation's founders, Beard argued, were not "isolationist," for "they were eager to promote commerce and intercourse with other nations." At the same time, they believed in "speaking softly, keeping the powder dry, withholding wrath except when war is intended as a last resort." Far from indifferent to the sufferings of others, Americans were surpassed by no people in aiding victims of war, famine, revolution, persecution, and earthquake.

The anti-interventionists possessed various assets upon which they could draw. First, they could call upon the entire American diplomatic tradition. George Washington's Farewell Address included a warning against "permanent alliances." Thomas Jefferson used the phrase "entangling alliances." According to the Monroe Doctrine, as embodied in President James Monroe's annual message of 1823, "In the wars of the European powers in matters relating to themselves we have never taken any part, nor does it comport with our policies to do so." Though many isolationists (but not all pacifists) were alarmed by Woodrow Wilson's call for U.S. membership in the League of Nations, they took comfort from Roosevelt's speech of 1936, delivered in Chautauqua, New York, where FDR called war profits "fool's gold" and pledged that he would "isolate" the nation from war.

Anti-interventionists could also draw upon majoritarian sentiment, for advocates of full-scale intervention were always in a clear minority. Only by opposing the president's policies, so foes of intervention claimed, could one implement the will of the 83 percent of the populace who, at the very height of prowar sentiment, opposed direct American entry in the conflict.

The Carriers of Anti-interventionism. Within the population, certain elements were particularly militant. If members of the House of Representatives at all reflect their constituency, one can point to a substantial cadre of anti-interventionist sentiment, based in particular in the Old Northwest and Great Plains states, but extending as well to the Border states, Pacific coast, rural Northeast, and even sections of northern cities. Then, despite defections by presidential candidate Wendell Willkie and various prominent eastern Republicans, the preponderance of sentiment in the Grand Old Party remained anti-interventionist.

Some occupational groups were centers of antiwar sentiment, and until well into 1940, one could find anti-administration sentiment disproportionally centered in students, farmers, and industrialists. Even when the Congress of Industrial Organizations (CIO) veered toward Roosevelt's foreign policy, its founder and most prominent member, John L. Lewis, staunchly opposed intervention. Protestant and Roman Catholic clergy differed among themselves on the issue, but many leading church periodicals remained suspicious of New Deal foreign policy. Certain ethnic groups housed strong anti-interventionist sentiments— in particular Americans of German, Irish, Italian, and possibly Scandinavian stock.

In addition, the anti-interventionists had significant vehicles with which to rally sentiment. Several giant newspaper chains fought Roosevelt until Pearl Harbor, including the Hearst, McCormick-Patterson, and Scripps-Howard combines. In 1939 Captain Joseph Patterson's liberal *New York Daily News* had a daily circulation of two million and three on Sunday, which made it not only the largest circulation in the

United States but third largest in the world. In 1941 Colonel Robert R. McCormick's *Chicago Tribune*, an arch-conservative paper, reached a million readers on weekdays, a million and a half on Sundays. Eleanor Medill ("Cissy") Patterson's pro-New Deal *Washington Times-Herald* was well on its way to having the largest circulation in the nation's capital. At the outset of the conflict such weekly magazines as the liberal *New Republic* and the conservative *Saturday Evening Post* were staunchly critical of FDR's policies. While the *New Republic* switched vehemently to the interventionist side in the summer of 1940, the *Atlantic Monthly*, *Harper's Magazine*, and the *Reader's Digest* welcomed anti-interventionist articles as much as interventionist ones to the very eve of American entry. The ultra-rightist monthly *Scribner's Commentator* opened its pages only to Roosevelt foes; its liberal and more urbane counterpart *Common Sense* retained anti-interventionist writers through the summer of 1941. The *Progressive*, published by the politically powerful La Follette family of Wisconsin, carried a host of anti-interventionist columnists. If the radio commentators and newscasters tended to be interventionist, adversaries presented their message through various radio forums and through an occasional commentator, such as Fulton Lewis, Jr., or Boake Carter, who also was a Hearst columnist. As far as individual leaders went, aviator Charles A. Lindbergh could match the charisma and magnetism of Roosevelt. Such anti-interventionist senators as Burton K. Wheeler (Dem.-Mont.), Gerald P. Nye (Rep.-N. D.), and Robert A. Taft (Rep.-Ohio) could never gain a congressional majority for their position, but offered articulate and impassioned arguments for their stance. Despite the bitter attacks upon them, anti-interventionists did not lack visibility.

As far as support among intellectuals went, the anti-interventionists were soon in a minority, though it was not a hopeless one. John Bassett Moore had written monumental legal studies and had served on the World Court. William Henry Chamberlin contributed the most respected history of the Russian Revolution of 1917. Harry Emerson Fosdick was the nation's most prominent Protestant radio preacher. Hubert Herring was a leading scholar of Latin America. Felix Morley was president of Haverford College; he had been chief editorial writer of the *Washington Post*.

On the left anti-interventionist sentiments were strong. The Socialist Party adopted an anti-interventionist platform (though one that caused the defection of many members), and its leader Norman Thomas was one of anti-interventionism's most respected proponents. From the sealing of the German-Russian pact of August 1939 to Hitler's invasion of the Soviet Union in June 1941, the Communist Party had similar sentiments. Not only did the New York *Daily Worker* praise such anti-interventionists as Senator Ernest Lundeen (Farmer-Labor-Minn.), a man to the left of the New Deal; such front journals as *Friday*, a competitor of *Life*, featured Beard's critique of the interventionist film "The Ramparts We Watch"; *US Week* warned against American convoys; and *New Masses* continually found Britain the arch-imperialist.

The non-democratic right was totally opposed to intervention. Highly visible was the German-American Bund, which patterned itself after Hitler's Nazi movement. Rallies included swastikas, banners, and uniforms. In reality the Bund was riddled with factionalism, recruited few German-Americans, and drew little support from the Nazi Party, the German state, and Hitler himself. Not surprisingly, however, the press gave it much play.

During the 1930s Father Charles E. Coughlin, a Roman Catholic priest from Royal Oak, Michigan, had been one of the most popular radio broadcasters in the entire world. In May 1940, he was forced off the air, his early calls for inflation and a silver standard having given way to anti-Semitism and pro-fascism. His weekly tabloid, *Social Justice*, reached less than 200,000 that year. Lawrence Dennis, who in 1935 wrote of a "desirable fascism" in his bulletin, the *Weekly Foreign Letter*, castigated the democracies for engaging in a destructive and futile struggle with the totalitarian powers.

When World War II broke out, anti-interventionist sentiment was diffuse and unorganized. There were only two broadly based anti-interventionist groups in existence, both somewhat pacifist in leaning. One was the National Council for the Prevention of War (NCPW), founded in 1921 by Quaker educator Frederick J. Libby as a clearing house for disarmament efforts. The NCPW served as an umbrella organization for a host of civic-minded groups that in 1940 ranged from the American section of the Women's International League for Peace and Freedom (WIL) and the Fellowship of Reconciliation (FOR) to the American Federation of Teachers and National Consumers' League. Libby determined all policy and member organizations were free to disagree. The NCPW had reached the peak of its influence in the mid-thirties, when it promoted both the Neutrality Acts (successfully) and a constitutional amendment to conduct a popular referendum before the United

States entered any war (unsuccessfully). By the time Hitler's panzers were crossing Poland, it had lost much ground to Roosevelt's interventionist policies and a host of affiliated bodies had withdrawn.

Second, there was the Keep America Out of War Congress (KAOWC), which from 1938 to the autumn of 1940 was the only national organization specifically created to oppose Roosevelt's foreign policy. It sought to unite trade unions, youth organizations, the Socialist Party, and peace groups (including the NCPW, the WIL, and the FOR) behind its program of strict neutrality and social reform. Day-to-day power was usually lodged in a permanent governing committee, composed of Socialist and pacifist leaders and usually meeting in New York. Its reformist position, far to the left of the New Deal, prevented the KAOWC from ever commanding mass support.

In September 1940, the America First Committee (AFC) was launched. Chaired by General Robert E. Wood, board chairman of Sears, Roebuck and backed heavily by midwestern business, the AFC mobilized the maximum amount of opposition possible to Roosevelt's policies. During the thirteen months of its existence, it held massive rallies, distributed tons of literature, sponsored national radio speakers, and supplied research data to members of Congress. By the time it folded, the AFC had 450 units and at least 800,000 members.

Europe Always at War. If the background of the anti-interventionist coalition was highly diverse, most shared the outlook articulated by Borah in his October 2 speech. To many anti-interventionists, Europe was always at war and would always be so. After all, they observed, the Old World had been one huge battleground since the fall of the Roman Empire. As Representative Louis Ludlow (Dem.-Ind.) remarked, "The Almighty created man with the traits of a fighting animal and there will always be wars." Senator Sheridan Downey (Dem.-Calif.) began his critique of cash-and-carry with the Battle of Hastings ("Mr. President, let us begin with 1066"). Congresswoman Frances P. Bolton (Rep-Ohio) listed each European war for a hundred years. The 1939 conflict was, to use the language of Charles A. Lindbergh, simply one "more of those age-old quarrels within our own family of nations."

World War I. Particularly haunting was the memory of World War I. An entire generation had been raised on revisionist histories that challenged a major wartime belief: the war had been caused by the Central

Powers and the Allies had been fighting for democracy. Harry Elmer Barnes's *The Genesis of the World War* (1926) and Sidney Bradshaw Fay's *Origins of the World War* (1928) found Germany less culpable than certain other belligerents, Austria and Russia among them. In an attempt to explain U.S. entry in 1917, Walter Millis's *Road to War* (1935) stressed the role of British propaganda, American banking, and such pro-Allied policymakers as presidential confidant Edward M. House and Secretary of State Robert Lansing. And, even if one was not an intellectual, the message conveyed by Ernest Hemingway's novel *A Farewell to Arms* (1929) and Lawrence Stallings's play *What Price Glory?* (1924) was quite simple: war was neither purposeful nor glorious. It was, as one character noted in John Dos Passos's *1919* (1932), "a goddamn madhouse." Writing from a pro-Communist perspective, Dalton Trumbo's novel *Johnny Got His Gun* (1939) interpreted combat through the recollections of a hospitalized veteran who had lost arms, legs, sight, and hearing. (*See Document No. 2.*)

In all this there were lessons. Ben Martin's *John Black's Body* (1939) used 48 pictures and 403 words to convey how war crushed the story of the "little man." James Thurber's *The Last Flower* (1939) showed the ensuing carnage reducing humanity to an animal state.

Versailles and the Subsequent Peace. If the horrors of the Great War were not enough, there were the political results. To anti-interventionists, the conflict had not produced a single significant aim of President Woodrow Wilson, neither satisfied nationalities nor tariff reduction nor freedom of the seas nor serious disarmament nor evacuation of the new Soviet state. Instead the "war to end wars," as British writer H. G. Wells had called it, was succeeded by new aggressions reaching from northern China to eastern Africa and by several dictatorships that genuinely deserved the label totalitarian. By 1934 Czechoslovakia was the only republic remaining in eastern Europe. Pacifist writer Milton Mayer told *Saturday Evening Post* readers in 1939, "We may compare the map of the world today with the map of 1914 and see at a glance just how much of the world was saved for democracy and how much lost." Representative Fred Bradley (Rep.-Mich.) commented, "We just burned our fingers to the bone, poking into a fire of European intrigue which had been smoldering for centuries."

The Versailles treaty symbolized the apparent betrayal of Wilsonianism. The whole document smacked of hatred and vindictiveness. Several million indigenous Germans were forced to live under alien rule. Reparation burdens appeared impossible. The Central Powers alone had to assume responsibility for causing all loss and damage resulting from "the aggression of Germany and her allies." Even in Asia, the virtual cession of a sphere of influence in Shantung, a thoroughly Chinese province, from Germany to Japan seemed a flagrant violation of the prime Wilsonian goal, the self-determination of peoples.

Former president Herbert Hoover, himself a participant at the famed Paris Conference, wrote a book *America's First Crusade* (1941) in which he said, "Destructive forces sat at the peace table. . . . Revenge for past wrongs rose every hour of the day." Senator Bennett Champ Clark (Dem.-Mo.) said, "Not since Rome punished Carthage was there such a treaty placed on any people." To Senator D. Worth Clark (Dem.-Idaho), France and England had surrounded Germany with "a ring of steel." More than one anti-interventionist drew a direct connection between the Paris Peace Conference—that "orgy in ink," as Senator Henrik Shipstead (Rep.-Minn.) called it—and the rise of Nazism. Commented pacifist spokesman Kirby Page, "If you sow a Versailles Treaty, you reap a Hitler."

To many anti-interventionists, the resulting League of Nations could never be an agent of genuine collective security. From its birth, it was simply an instrument of the victors to preserve the status quo. Because the League Covenant had made ample provision for peaceful change, Wilson had seen the organization as the one body able to rectify any wrongs embodied in the Paris treaties. To American anti-interventionists, however, the League smacked more of Clemens von Metternich's Holy Alliance than of any true "parliament of man." U.S. membership in that body, it was argued, would not only have forced it to take part in every quarrel in the world; it would have made it an accomplice in Allied supremacy everywhere. Shipstead called it "the refrigerator in which the plans of the 'peace' treaty framers were to be preserved."

Many of these themes were articulated by historian Howard K. Beale, a staunch pacifist, civil libertarian, and specialist in the American Civil War and Reconstruction. Beale denied that ideas, even National Socialist ones, could be defeated on the battlefield and that Hitler was chiefly responsible for the outbreak of World War II. (*See Document No. 3.*)

Munich. To some anti-interventionists, the Munich conference of September 1938 had proven the perfidy of Europe's diplomats. Nothing else so revealed the treachery of France and Britain as depriving Czechoslovakia of its one defensible frontier. To Gerald P. Nye, Hitler was being "bought off"; to Hugh Johnson, Czechoslovakia was being "thrown to the wolves." Senator Rush Holt accused British prime minister Neville Chamberlain of selling the Czechs "down the river." "And do not worry," the West Virginia Democrat continued, "they [the British] will sell any country in the world down the river when British imperialism is at stake."

For other anti-interventionists, Munich was both necessary and wise. Britain was buying needed time, they argued, for in 1938 it was unprepared for any war. Asked Joseph P. Kennedy, U.S. ambassador to Britain and father of President John F. Kennedy, "Can anyone imagine what would have happened to England if the 'blitzkrieg' of the summer of 1940 had occurred in September of 1938?" At the time of Munich, noted General Robert E. Wood, England had only seven aircraft bombers.

Besides, some anti-interventionists found Britain and France prudent in attempting to channel Germany's expansion eastward. According to William Henry Chamberlin, foreign correspondent for the *Christian Science Monitor*, France had missed its one opportunity to crush Germany single-handedly by permitting Germany to invade the Rhineland in 1936. Now there was only one reasonable policy left: to hope for an ultimate clash between the Third Reich and the Soviet Union.

But on August 23, 1939 German foreign minister Joachim von Ribbentrop dashed all such expectations by making a non-aggression pact with his Soviet counterpart Vyacheslav Molotov. Included in the agreement was a secret provision dividing Eastern Europe between the two powers. Within ten days a new world war had begun.

CHAPTER 2

WAR BREAKS OUT

Invasion of Poland. On September 1, 1939 Adolf Hitler attacked Poland. Though he claimed to be primarily concerned with Danzig and the corridor, a small parcel of territory that gave Poland unhindered access to the Baltic Sea, he had long made clear to his approving generals that he sought far more territory. On September 3, after the Führer refused appeals to pull back, the British and French declared war on Germany. Within hours after they entered the conflict, Roosevelt gave one of his famous "fireside chats," in which the president pledged that "every effort of government" would be aimed at keeping "out of this war." On September 5, FDR invoked the Neutrality Act, closing American arsenals to belligerents.

Sympathy for Poland. By mid-September Poland was defeated. On September 17, the Soviets invaded from the east, claiming their share of that nation.

Some anti-interventionists expressed real sympathy for Poland. Oswald Garrison Villard, a prominent liberal who formerly published the *Nation* magazine, wrote: "Theirs is the righteous cause; they were willing to negotiate; the records show that Hitler went around lying and in haste. The horrible odium of having induced this war is his." Herbert Hoover launched a fullscale campaign to feed starving Poles, which included speaking at rallies, writing articles, and testifying before Congress. "There will be no permanent peace," he said, "and therefore no stability in the world as long as oppression of a great and independent race continues in Poland." General Hugh Johnson pointed to the German execution of Jews in Warsaw and Roman Catholic landlords in German and Russian areas, something—he said—not equaled since Genghis Khan and Attila. Charles A. Lindbergh studiously and consistently avoided any public condemnation of Germany, doing so on the grounds that it would fan war flames. Yet he publicly claimed to be "very much opposed to what happened in the German invasion of Poland." *Social Justice*, published by Father Charles E. Coughlin, was often pro-fascist, but this weekly tabloid referred to "Christian Poland's assassination" and accused Hitler of lending himself to "the pagan plottings" of the anti-Christ.

Polish Misconduct. Yet other anti-interventionists stressed that Poland's own record was far from spotless. Indeed they found Poland a backward, reactionary, bigoted despotism. Why were there no civil liberties once General Joseph Pilsudski took over in 1926? Why, until the rise of Hitler, did Poland hold first place in anti-Semitic barbarism? Hearst columnist Boake Carter claimed that in 1938, Poland had destroyed 114 Orthodox churches and had seized 186 Ukrainian churches, doing so in the hopes of destroying the Ukrainian nationalist movement.

Then there was the matter of Poland's conduct in Europe. The *Christian Century*, a liberal Protestant weekly, accused Poland of attacking Galicia even before the Paris Peace Conference of 1919 had adjourned; within a year it invaded Russia. Just after the Munich conference, it seized 7,000 square miles of Czech territory. As Congressman John Marshall Robsion (Rep.-Kt.) saw the issue, "Poland grabbed last year, and was grabbed herself this year." Economist John T. Flynn concurred, calling Poland "almost the first of the vultures to swoop down upon the disintegrating carcass."

German Case over Danzig and the Corridor. When it came to the publicly articulated demands over Danzig and the Corridor, several anti-interventionists claimed that Germany was in the right. As Hugh Johnson saw it, Danzig was a German city, the Polish Corridor a monstrosity. Morally, said Yale law professor Edwin M. Borchard, Hitler "has a good case." Britain, so Senator William J. Bulow (Dem.-S. D.) claimed, should have permitted the people of that city ("who were Germans and formerly belonged to the German Reich") to reunite with their mother country.

Occasionally memories reached back to the 1919 Paris peace conference. Congressman Robsion recalled that President Woodrow Wilson had once issued a warning: depriving Germany of Danzig and the Corridor would bring on another war. He asked, "Who wants to send two or three American boys to Europe to help take Danzig from Germany and give it back to Poland?" The *Christian Century* noted the famous Fontainebleu memorandum of Prime Minister David Lloyd George to French premier Georges Clemenceau. Dated March 25, 1919, it warned that putting German nationals under foreign rule would lead to hostilities.

Moreover, several anti-interventionists found irresponsible the British-French guarantee to Poland, made on March 30, 1939. To Hugh Johnson, Britain's declaration of war was "one of the greatest and most stupid blunders in history—if not the greatest." Bruce Barton, advertising executive and Republican congressman representing Manhattan's "silk-stocking" district, claimed that a simple look at a map could show that it was impossible for the two allies to come to Poland's aid.

The Lindberghs were particularly concerned. A week before the conflict began, Charles Lindbergh confided to his diary, "Poland is beyond help under any circumstances. The German Army alone will close the Corridor within a few days after it attacks, and there is no other way for England and France to get to Poland." Rather than declare war, said Charles, Britain and France "should have built their strength and safety behind the Maginot line and the British fleet." His wife concurred. The prominent poet Anne Morrow Lindbergh declared two weeks before war, England "will fight, I think, even if it is mass suicide. Is this courage or is it stupidity?" When war broke out, she predicted the German conquest of Poland and the merciless bombing of London and Paris. "It will be a new Spain," she said, referring to the recent bloody conflict in that land.

To some degree, all anti-interventionists agreed with Robert A. Taft, one of the more moderate figures in their ranks. The Ohio Republican claimed to sympathize with Poland, but found "no reason why we should run on the field and play quarterback." The *Chicago Tribune* noted that the United States had not created the Danzig situation; it had no stake in it.

Roosevelt Proposes Cash-and-Carry. On September 21, Roosevelt, sympathetic to Britain and France, addressed a special session of the Congress. He asked it to revise the existing Neutrality law, one that had prohibited all sales of munitions overseas. FDR's proposal was tied to another requirement—namely that all such purchases be strictly for cash and be transported in foreign vessels. In fact, buyers of American goods must take title before leaving the United States. American ships, he continued, must be banned from entering "the actual zones of conflict." The president did not acknowledge what was obvious to *Time* magazine, namely that the current U.S. embargo "gave

Adolf Hitler almost the equivalent of an Atlantic fleet, because Great Britain and France can get no arms from the U.S." Rather he presented his proposal as a peace measure, stressing that "cash-and-carry" should, if enforced, prevent the torpedoing of American vessels and avert destruction of American property in combat zones.

The administration skillfully mobilized public opinion. William Allan White, editor and publisher of the *Emporia* (Kansas) *Gazette*, chaired the Non-Partisan Committee for Peace through Revision of the Neutrality Act, a body far more effective than the relative diffuse efforts of the bill's opponents. Even some figures later vocal in their anti-interventionism went along. Senator Taft, for example, denied that repeal of the arms embargo increased American chances of getting into war. Besides, he continued, it was "Pharisaical" for the United States to supply steel, machinery, nitrates, and cotton while claiming that "our hands are too clean to complete the process of manufacture." The *New York Daily News* called the current practice "a help to Hitler."

Opposition Arguments. The battle over Roosevelt's proposal lasted four weeks minus one day. During this time, some seventy senators contributed over a million words.

For some opponents memories of World War I were strong. Bruce Barton feared a repetition of early 1917, when American ships had been sunk even before the nation entered the conflict. "The German people," he said, "had been made insane with anger because it was our guns, our shells, our gas, and our airplanes that were murdering their sons."

Any focus on cash, claimed other anti-interventionists, was strictly a pipedream. Eventually the Allies would run out of hard currency. Once they did so, they would seek loans, just as they had in 1915 and 1916. At first the United States, still in economic depression, would experience a tremendous war boom. In time, however, the prosperity would lead to a severe inflation. Within four years, warned Senator Downey, government credit would fall, the administration would be forced to declare an emergency, and the state would seize factories and farms.

In the meantime, the American economy would become dependent upon the Allied cause. Warned Nye, "When industry after industry is operating on war orders, expanding their debts and their plants to fill war orders, when millions of farmers are mortgaging themselves to the hilt to grow food and cotton at war prices, when the British Empire is permitted to assume the terrible risk of war conquest on the basis of our supplies—then we have created what I mean by economic involvement."

Journalist C. Hartley Grattan wrote a book containing such warnings. Here he claimed that selling "American guns" to Britain and France would strengthen popular sentiment for the Allied cause just as similar arms traffic had done in World War I. In time every barrier to intervention would be lowered. The title of his work: *The Deadly Parallel* (1939).

Others concurred. "If a man doesn't take the first drink of liquor, he will never get intoxicated," said Representative Thomas B. Miller (Rep.-Pa.). For Senator Bennett Champ Clark, cash-and-carry would soon be followed by "crash and carry," and in the long run by "clash and carry." The Scripps-Howard chain found the United States "starting out on an airplane ride, without giving thought to taking along a parachute, when we know we are going to need it."

There were other dangers as well. Senator Vandenberg envisioned a foreign ship, loaded with prepaid contraband, being sunk on the high seas. If the incident occurred up to three hundred miles out to sea, the United States might become involved in a sticky controversy over the limits of its territorial waters. And, some warned, even if American ships were not sunk, there was the danger of sabotage. Americans might expect buildings to be bombed, subways dynamited, bridges blown up, ships sunk, water polluted.

Another line of argument centered on America's own munitions shortages. The United States could profitably meet its own military munitions needs, it was claimed, without having to sell a nickel's worth overseas. Congressman Thomas C. Martin (Rep.-Iowa) asked, "Who are we to talk of selling armament abroad when at present our Army has only one brigade that is mechanized?" Furthermore, there was no guarantee of any European market. FDR's critics argued that Britain and France possessed plenty of munitions already and moreover could manufacture war implements far more cheaply than could the United States.

To some anti-interventionists, the very idea of sending munitions to any side seemed immoral, for it meant that some Americans were profiting from the tragedy of others. Terms were used like "unholy business," "blood money," "international sadism," "cash-and-bury," and Roosevelt's own term in the Chautauqua address—"fool's gold." Congressman Hamilton Fish (Rep.-N.Y.), representing FDR's own district on the Hudson, asked whether the lives of Americans "boys" must be risked for "30 pieces of silver" so that some Americans might "reap a harvest of war profits." Smedley Butler, a former marine general who had practically become a pacifist, warned, "The American people are about to buy another international goldbrick." Butler even found the sale of toothpicks dangerous: "toothpicks are merely cellulose in splinter form."

Still another factor is most surprising in retrospect—the attention paid by certain anti-interventionists to international law. In his September 21 speech, Roosevelt opened the issue himself, for he claimed that he was merely returning to "the age-old and time-honored doctrine of international law," which permitted neutrals to trade with belligerents in "goods and products of all kinds."

Two law professors from Columbia University, Philip C. Jessup and Charles Cheney Hyde, responded immediately. The United States, they claimed, could possibly expose itself to brutal retaliation if Germany won the war. Furthermore, it was emulating Hitler by its breaking down the rules of international law.

Professor Borchard had written often on this subject. Indeed he was coauthor of a massive work *Neutrality for the United States* (1937; rev. 1940). According to the Yale scholar, a nation could not legally relax its neutrality, with the motive or even the effect of aiding one belligerent. While Borchard had opposed embargoes and boycotts in any form, he maintained that only one kind of change could be made during wartime: that of tightening a nation's neutrality. (*See Document No. 4.*)

Protest reached far beyond elements of the scholarly community. Would Roosevelt have made his plea, queried Congressman James W. Mott (Rep.-Ore.), if it had been the Nazi government that held the wide edge in naval ships and merchant vessels? Congressman George A. Dondero (Rep.-Mich.) remarked, "If two men are fighting in the street, and you are standing nearby, and give one of them a knife, are you neutral?" Fish, once all-American tackle for Harvard, compared the change to "changing the rules after the kick-off in a football game."

Anti-interventionist Alternatives. Several anti-interventionists sought to weaken this legislation. Senator Charles W. Tobey (Rep.-N. H.) proposed an amendment that would have retained the arms embargo while allowing cash-and-carry for other goods. Herbert Hoover sought to ban any export of "offensive weapons," by which he meant bombers, poison gas, and submarines. On the other hand, the United States would be permitted to ship pursuit planes, light observation planes, and antiaircraft guns. Charles A. Lindbergh concurred: "I do not want to see American bombers dropping bombs which will kill and mutilate European children, even if they are not flown by American pilots. But I am perfectly willing to see American antiaircraft guns shooting American shells at invading bombers over any European country."

Cash-and-carry, however, passed both houses easily and was signed by Roosevelt on November 4. The president's position was supported by a Gallup poll taken in mid-September, which showed 62 percent in favor of repealing the arms embargo. At first, however, the Allies placed few orders for American supplies. Reasons included a standstill in fighting, the desire to protect their own gold and dollar reserves, and the belief that the conflict could last three years, thereby giving France and Britain sufficient time to produce more arms.

Invasion of Finland. Though Congress ended up passing cash-and-carry by a comfortable margin, America's dilemmas were just beginning, for, on November 30, the Soviet Union launched a full-scale attack on Finland. Russian warships shelled the Finnish coast, its bombers raiding Helsinki.

Yet, for three months, it appeared as if the Finns might be able to repel the invasion, at least if they received material and volunteers from outside. Roosevelt strongly condemned the invasion, explored various ways of aiding Finland, and finally decided upon a loan program. He permitted some loans on his own authority, then asked Congress for more funds. The Senate Banking Committee proposed a token loan of $20 million, out of which Finland could buy trucks, raw materials, and agricultural goods. The Finns could not, however, buy what they really needed, which was arms.

Endorsement of Aid to Finland. Among the general American population, anti-interventionists included, there was far more sympathy for the Finns than for the Poles. The liberal Roman Catholic weekly *Commonweal* put the issue best: "Americans particularly cannot help having deep sympathy for the Finns. We have heard so much about them that appeals to us; their sturdy independence, their development of cooperatives, their steadfast payments to us on their debt." Congressman William A. Pittenger (Rep.-Minn.), obviously casting an eye to constituents of Scandinavian descent, warned that if Finland fell, Sweden, Norway, and Denmark would be next. Finland, he continued, "is fighting the battle of all civilized countries." To Frank C. Waldrop, foreign and political editor of the *Washington Times-Herald*, "There is just one real issue. Which is the greater risk to the United States—to give Finland genuine support or let Russia build her power to the Atlantic?"

Anti-interventionists Dissent. Many anti-interventionists, however, opposed the loans. To Borchard, such a government loan was an illegal act exposing the United States to legitimate reprisals from the Soviets. Commented Senator Alva Adams (Dem.-Colo.), "We can't save Finland by going to war with Russia."

Particularly fearsome was the precedent. All kinds of phrases were used—"the Trojan horse of intervention," the "camel's nose under the tent," "the new Belgium"—the latter phrase an obvious comparison to sympathies engendered in the Great War. Loans to other belligerents were bound to follow. Clyde Reed (Rep.-Kan.) felt that even the Netherlands and Switzerland would be in on the take. Had the United States not lent money during World War I, claimed Senator Pat McCarran (Dem.-Nev.), "we should not have row on row of white crosses in Flanders fields." There was also the issue of domestic priorities. Senator Holt said, "If we have $100,000,000, there are thousands of hungry, naked and homeless Americans who could use part of that money."

Additional Proposals. Anti-interventionists made additional proposals. Hoover, for example, wanted to sever diplomatic relations with the Soviets. Indeed, 105 members of the House voted to withhold funds for the salary of the American ambassador to Moscow. There was also the possibility of cutting off all trade. At the time American copper, tools, dies, and machines were being routed to Siberia, for obvious use by the Red Army. "I can see headlines from here," said Senator Robert Rice Reynolds (Dem.-N. C.). "The Finns are complaining that American airplanes are being used to kill people." One could also support private aid to Finland. The ubiquitous Hoover, for instance, established the Finnish Relief Fund, which amassed some $2.5 million.

The debate, however, soon became academic, for on March 12, the Finns were forced to sign a peace, one that involved the ceding of strategic areas, rich forest, 10 percent of their arable land, and 625 miles of railroad.

CHAPTER 3

AN ALTERNATIVE PERSPECTIVE

Pro-Allied Sentiments. During all this time, anti-interventionists were forming general perspectives on the entire conflict. Though many anti-interventionists blamed the rise of Nazism first on Versailles, then on Allied appeasement, few desired a German victory. "No one," said Senator Hiram Johnson (Rep.-Calif.), "could wish more ardently than I do for the defeat of Hitler." Senator Wheeler expressed horror over Nazi treatment of Germany's Jews. A. J. Muste, the FOR's (Fellowship for Reconciliation) executive secretary, commented, "I do not want to minimize the evil of a German victory. I recoil from every prospect of it." Senator Taft found himself detesting every action taken by the German government since Hitler assumed power. To former president Hoover, the sufferings of occupied Europe "cry out to the sympathy of every decent man and woman."

Similarly most anti-interventionists were sympathetic to England, hoping that Britain would hold off the Nazi onslaught. Hoover saw no contradiction in the statements, "I am for aid to Britain. I am against naval or military intervention in this war." Hence the great majority expressed support of Britain, even at times going so far as to boast of British ancestry. Wheeler remarked, "No blood but English flows through my veins. And next to being pro-American I am pro-English."

Propaganda Feared. Yet, despite pro-Allied sympathies, anti-interventionists continually warned against Propaganda— often used with a capital P—as a physician warns against disease. Alert citizens, they claimed, must be able to detect it instantly and thereby be able to quarantine themselves against it. Actress Lillian Gish saw danger in uncritical acceptance of atrocity stories. Recalling her travels in wartorn England in 1917, she remembered being asked on her return if the Germans "cut off the hands and legs of old people and crucified little children."

In an article in *Collier's* printed in March 1941, Charles A. Lindbergh accused the British of deliberately misleading Americans on a number of matters. (*See Document No. 5.*) Most of his claims were particularly significant—and closely watched— as the prominent aviator was increasingly becoming the anti-interventionist's leading drawing card, the only public figure whose popular appeal might match the president's. Yet as one of the more extreme of the anti-interventionists, Lindbergh denied wanting either Germany or Britain to win the war. He refused to return a Nazi decoration unexpectedly bestowed upon him in 1938, would not condemn German atrocities publicly, and— writing for the *Reader's Digest* in 1939—called for building "our White ramparts." A "Western wall of race and arms," he said in the November issue, could hold back "either a Genghis Khan or the infiltration of inferior blood," and he spoke of the common role that could be played by "an English fleet, a German air force, a French army, an American nation." In late August 1941, Lindbergh warned that Great Britain itself might turn against the United States.

An Imperialist War. Many anti-interventionists saw the initial conflict not as a war to preserve democracy, but rather an imperialist war, one between two predatory blocs of nations. In short, to some the war was not between good and evil but between competing evils. Said historian Eric F. Goldman of Johns Hopkins University, "I don't believe this is a war of ideologies. It is merely one of a series of age-old struggles of European nations striving to preserve their hegemonies." Socialist leader Norman Thomas commented, "The cross over Europe today is not the cross seen by Constantine the Great but the double cross."

Historian and sociologist Harry Elmer Barnes found the conflict centering on "the old thieves" versus "the new thieves." Barnes was midway in a career that would ultimately end with him denying German responsibility for starting World War II and the existence of Hitler's "final solution." Yet at this stage he was a firm liberal, whose causes included penal reform, civil liberties, and a welfare state. (*See Document No. 6.*)

However, when it came to defining the precise nature of this imperialism, the foes of intervention differed. Some stressed the balance of power. Senator Bulow, for example, found the war centering on "who shall boss the job of establishing national boundaries on the continent of Europe."

In an article written in the *Atlantic Monthly* of March 1940, Charles A. Lindbergh saw the conflict as "a continuation of the old struggle among western nations for the material benefits of the world." The Germans sought to "conquer territory and influence by force of arms as other nations have done at one time or another throughout history." The French and British wanted to maintain "their possessions and their ethics, and the status quo of their last victory." Hence, he continued, "This war in Europe is not so much a conflict between right and wrong as it is a conflict between differing concepts of right—a conflict in which the 'defenders' are represented by static, legal 'right' of man, and the 'aggressors' by the dynamic, forceful 'right' of nature. No nation," he continued, "has been consistent in its concept of either," referring to France during the time of Napoleon and Britain during the Boer War.

Others emphasized geographical empire. Nye found it comparable to "the long imperial war by which England ousted France from world empire, and, before that, France ousted Spain." The newsletter *Uncensored*, produced by liberals within isolationist ranks, mentioned "control of native populations in Africa, Asia and Europe." Sociologist Edward A. Ross saw the issue as one of colonies, saying "Germany got tired of this hogging of world space by Britain."

John Haynes Holmes, minister of the New York Community Church, was a militant reformer who had long fought intolerance against Jews and blacks. Holmes not only stressed "the age-old struggle for military predominance and imperialistic rule"; he claimed that other peoples had first invented the crimes that Hitler was committing. (*See Document No. 7.*)

A few anti-interventionists found economic rivalries at the heart of the matter. For example, James D. Mooney, president of the General Motors Overseas Corporation, saw Germany and Italy "fighting and striving to keep from being starved to death." Both nations felt that England and France controlled the commodities, raw materials, and trade of the world; hence their own food supply, resources, and markets were being throttled.

Perceived German War Aims. Most anti-internationists denied that Hitler sought world conquest. To pacifist leader Frederick J. Libby, the German Führer sought to end "British domination of the world" by domination of Suez, Gibraltar, and other strategic points. The *Chicago Tribune* stressed Germany's desire for permanent rule of Poland and economic leadership in southeastern Europe. John T. Flynn saw the Reich's ultimate goals centering on Romania and the Ukraine. Publisher William Randolph Hearst concretely denied that Germany wanted world domination; rather it sought, a United States of Europe and conquest of the Soviet Union. General Wood found Hitler's *Mein Kampf* (1925) outlining a program for German expansion in Europe, not the Western Hemisphere.

Even if the Germans did seek world domination, anti-interventionists denied that they could ever achieve it. Wheeler found Hitler's talk along such lines no more impressive than earlier boasts of Lenin and Trotsky concerning world revolution. The *New York Daily News* predicted that Nazi-occupied Europe would "begin coming unglued as soon as Hitler's Nazism shows itself unable to make life comfortably livable for most people under its hooked-cross banner."

Critique of Allied War Goals. Conversely, so anti-interventionists maintained, the Allies had no positive war aims. They only sought the defeat and partition of Germany, a Carthaginian peace bound to create more dictators and more wars of revenge. Publisher Oswald Garrison Villard, like Holmes an outspoken reformer, was particularly concerned about the French, who—he wrote in December 1939—sought to split Germany into Catholic and Protestant states. To the *New York Daily News*, the French wanted to annex Germany "right up to the Rhine," then break up the rest of the country into several small units.

Several anti-interventionists were particularly fearful of the economic aims of the British. Senator McCarran called "the question abroad" a question of commercial supremacy, of whether "unified powers within the center of Europe shall prevail against the British Empire." Hearst saw England fighting to protect its economic dominance and hence world domination, which—he said—were the very same aims it had in World War I, not to mention in the Napoleonic wars.

If most anti-interventionists had nothing but sympathy for the British cause, some of the more vocal blasted the British at every opportunity. Prime minister Neville Chamberlain and foreign minister Lord Halifax were portrayed as the architects of Munich, British ambassador Lord Lothian as a confidant of Hitler. Chamberlain's successor, Winston Churchill, received perhaps the greatest abuse of all, as his entire military and civil career was seen as a combination of blunder and reaction. Hearst was kinder than many, in fact, in referring to him as "a well-meaning eloquent-speaking old gentleman"!

The issue of Britain, however, transcended personalities. Anti-interventionists brought up the Düsseldorf agreements of 1939, by which the Federation of British Industries sought to collaborate with powerful German counterparts in capturing varied markets, including those of the United States. Other administration critics denied that Britain was still a democracy, if it had ever been one; rather it was a wartime dictatorship with centralized powers equaling those of Hitler. For Britain's critics, evidence included press censorship, lengthening of working hours, fixing of wages, and postponement of parliamentary elections. The British government could tell its citizens how much meat they could eat, how late their homes could stay open, indeed whether their children must be evacuated to the countryside or remain at home.

The empire proved to be a popular target. Hardly an area flying the Union Jack escaped anti-interventionist scrutiny. Indeed it appeared as if throughout history Britain had been the very mother of oppression. Although Palestine and Africa were occasionally brought up, India and Ireland were the regions most frequently mentioned. D. Worth Clark cited Edmund Burke's indictment of Warren Hastings, governor general of India at the time of the American Revolution, then went on to claim that the British record in Ireland was ten times as savage as Germany's current persecutions! Nye saw Britain carrying on its activity as "the ace aggressor of all time." (*See Document No. 8.*) Asked Hugh Johnson, "Is Britain fighting our war?" and he answered with a resounding no. (*See Document No. 9.*)

Fear of American Imperialism. According to some anti-interventionists, the United States itself could become an imperialistic power. Those of the left particularly stressed this factor. *Uncensored* accused the United States of seeking a huge customs union, one run from Washington and including all Latin America and the British Dominions. A. J. Muste said, "It seems clearer each day that we shall be the next nation to seek world-domination—in other words, to do what we condemn Hitler for trying to do."

But the left was not alone. Roosevelt's former braintruster Raymond Moley, who wrote a column for *Newsweek*, asked, "Are we going to be a nation or an empire?" Senator George Aiken (Rep.-Vt.) attacked those interventionists who "envision their flag waving in glory over the oil fields of Asia Minor and the plantations of the East Indies."

In general, so anti-interventionists argued, any such imperialist aims were unattainable. Senator Taft wondered what the United States would do with eighty million Germans. Flynn feared that the United States would be policing Europe for a hundred years. During the lend-lease debate, Stuart Chase, an economist who always sought a planned society, saw the United States bearing an impossible burden. (*See Document No. 10.*) Before the United States ever reached such a stage, however, it had more immediate problems to confront, those centering on northern Europe.

CHAPTER 4

AN EMERGENCY QUESTIONED

The End of the Phony War. During the winter of 1939–1940, so little activity existed on the Western front that the conflict became known as the "phony war." The phrase originated with Senator Borah who said in October 1939, "there is something phony about this war." One limerick went: "A elderly man with gout/ When asked what this war was about/ Replied with a sigh/ My colleagues and I/ Are doing our best to find out."

All changed, however, when in the early dawn of April 9, 1940, German columns moved across the Danish border. By noon, the entire nation was occupied. Simultaneously, German warships appeared in the fjord leading to Oslo, German planes flew over the Norwegian capital, and German troops took over such posts as Bergen, Trondhjem, Stavanger, and Narvik.

Like the rest of America, most anti-interventionists were horrified. Anne Morrow Lindbergh commented, "I felt that familiar sick-at-the-pit-of-the-stomach shock that all moves of Germany give instinctively to you." Yet for many foes of intervention, blame was placed squarely on the English. To them, it was the British mining of Norwegian waters, a clear violation of that country's neutrality, that triggered the German attack.

Even more significant action took place on May 10, for Hitler launched his main attack on the Allies through Belgium and the Netherlands. The Dutch capitulated in five days, the Belgians in eighteen, the French in forty-three. By late May, the Germans were already at the English Channel. Soon a huge air battle was being waged over English skies, the famous "Battle of Britain." There were many predictions that Hitler would soon launch a ground invasion of that embattled isle.

Roosevelt permitted government-owned armaments to be sold to private interests, who in turn would resell them to the British. On June 10, 1940, in a speech at Charlottesville, Virginia, he pledged "to the opponents of force the material resources of this nation," thereby abandoning all pretense of neutrality. The president also took a slap at Mussolini's Italy, which had just attacked France. "The hand that held the dagger," he said, "has struck it in the back of its neighbor."

To all Americans, anti-interventionists included, the invasion was jolting. The *Christian Century* claimed that Germany's action "has profoundly shocked the moral sense of a world which has believed itself almost beyond shock." Charles A. Lindbergh said to his wife, "I can't keep those troops out of my mind. I know what hell is going on there, what hell." Hiram Johnson found Hitler marching into Paris "a horrible thing to contemplate." William Henry Chamberlin compared the fall of Paris to that of Constantinople in 1453. Herbert Hoover spoke in terms of the sack of Rome by the barbarian king, Alaric in 410 A.D. Indeed, to the former president, the world was experiencing "the most gigantic drama of 1,000 years."

The President's Warnings. On May 16, just as the Allied armies were beginning to retreat from Belgium to France, Roosevelt delivered a message to Congress calling for the production of at least 50,000 military planes a year. Warning against aerial attack, the president presented some frightening scenarios: it took only seven hours flying time from Cape Verde islands to Brazil; four hours from Brazil to Caracas, Venezuela; two and half hours from Caracas to Cuba and the Canal Zone; another two and a quarter hours from Cuba and the Canal Zone to Tampico, Mexico; two and a quarter hours from Tampico to St. Louis, Kansas City, and Omaha. Similar scenarios were sketched concerning attack via Alaska, Greenland, and the Azores.

Ten days later, FDR gave a "fireside chat" to the nation. Here he took credit for defense moves already made while stressing the need for far greater mobilization. He warned against "the fifth column that betrays a nation unprepared for treachery" and attacked those who had "closed their eyes to events abroad." Congress responded to the president's pleas by voting him an additional 1.2 billion dollars for defense. It also attempted to ward off subversion by legislation making it unlawful to advocate or teach the overthrow of the U.S. government by force and violence.

War Hysteria. Yet, as France fell, many Americans were more jittery than ever. In Brooklyn, a war-crazed British sailor danced despairingly on a high window ledge. In Manhattan and Seattle, two men killed themselves because of the news. New York's colorful mayor Fiorello La Guardia griped that the United States could not even protect Coney Island.

Danger, it seemed, was everywhere. A foundry worker, disliking the taste of some water given him by a friend, killed the man as a traitor. Illinois farmers demanded antitank guns to protect their cornfields. The mayor of San Antonio equipped his police force with machine guns to mow down any fifth-columnists approaching from Mexico. Sixty members of a gun club in Pittsburgh sought official status as antiparachute troopers. Conversely the city manager of a town in Texas warned people against taking shots at any parachutist; it might be an American trainee practicing bailing out. Navaho Indians banned subversive activities among tribe members.

Anti-interventionists were appalled at what they deemed deliberate scare tactics. According to the *Christian Century*, Roosevelt was making "many a citizen feel as though a German bombing plane might be flying over his home by morning." Advertising executive Chester Bowles noted the panic over "the possibility of German parachutists capturing New York City Hall and blowing up Boulder Dam." Congressman Fish asked, "Why every time an automobile backfires the people of Washington should envision the panzer divisions marching up Pennsylvania Avenue?" Soon, he continued, the administration would be "asking for submarines in the Dust Bowls." Such anxieties carried over to the Pacific as well. Wheeler continually heard that the Japanese were about to attack the major cities of the West Coast: San Francisco, Los Angeles, Seattle, and Portland.

A Scenario Challenged. Until the time the Japanese attacked Pearl Harbor, anti-interventionists continually challenged Roosevelt's scenario. *Uncensored* conceded Roosevelt's claim that the Azores were only 2,000 miles from parts of our eastern seaboard, but denied that any bomber could fly 2,000 miles, drop a bomb load, and return to its base. Charles A. Lindbergh, whose name was practically synonymous with the rise of American aviation, found the advantage lying with the United States. (*See Document No. 11.*)

In 1941 military expert Hanson Baldwin offered a detailed account of why the nation could not be attacked. In his book *United We Stand!* (1941), he spoke of "the bogey of invasion." (*See Document No. 12.*) In anti-interventionist eyes, the fact that Baldwin wrote for a leading interventionist paper, the *New York Times*, made his case all the more credible.

Burke-Wadsworth Introduced. Yet despite such reassurances, it was hardly surprising that within days after France fell, two members of Congress introduced a conscription bill. Senator Edward R. Burke (Dem.-Neb.) and Congressmen James S. Wadsworth (Rep.-N.Y.), both fervent anti-New Dealers, called for registering all men between twenty-one and forty-five, a category involving some forty million, for possible military training. Eventually, men between twenty-one and thirty-one would be liable for selection.

The bill was a most decisive step. At first Roosevelt himself was a bit vague about supporting the proposal. On July 19, however, in accepting the Democratic nomination for president, he asserted that "some form of selection by draft is as fair and necessary today as it was in 1917 and 1918." Two weeks later, at a press conference, he forthrightly endorsed "a selective training bill." The United States, said FDR, did not just need weapons; it needed the trained men to use them. He went on: "You cannot get a sufficiently trained force of all kinds at the front, in the navy yards and the arsenals, transportation, supply system, and munitions output, you cannot get it just by passing an Act of Congress when war breaks out, and you cannot get it by the mere volunteer system." Hence immediate conscription was needed. General George C. Marshall, army chief of staff, backed FDR fully.

A few anti-interventionists favored the move. For example, General Hugh Johnson, who had written major provisions of the selective service act in 1917, offered an "isolationist" argument in favor of the draft: it would help create an impregnable America. He said in a radio broadcast, "With our strength of men and resources we can take a defensive position which nobody will ever dare threaten." Even before the bill was introduced, Charles A. Lindbergh had endorsed at least one year's military training for each male. In late August the *New York Daily News* fearing that Britain's defeat could be imminent, hoped that there still might "be time to collect and train an army of men whose brutal instincts will be attuned to the brutal machines of Twentieth Century war."

Arguments Against Conscription. For a few anti-interventionists, the bill was one of the most dangerous ever introduced in the halls of Congress. Senator Homer T. Bone (Dem.-Wash.) was not alone in warning, "Upon this vote hinges the ultimate destiny of this Republic."

Some arguments were military, centering on the claim that the danger was insufficient, the means unnecessary. Congressman Fish saw no need to raise huge numbers of troops when the United States already possessed the largest navy in the world, indeed one seven times the strength of the Germans, and an air force expanding at the potential rate of 800 planes a week. *Uncensored* doubted if "a murderous marauder, baffled by the English Channel, would find the Atlantic Ocean a duck pond." Such a move only made sense, said Hanson Baldwin, if the United States was preparing for "a death struggle with a Japanized Asia and a completely Germanized Europe in which all the navies and merchant marine and ship-building facilities on the continent were in German hands."

Moreover, so argued administration foes, the existing war showed just how outmoded mass conscript armies were. Germany's recent victory in France revealed the supremacy of relatively small cadres of elite corps, trained in tank warfare, against legions of French *poilus*. Senator David I. Walsh (Dem.-Mass.) noted that 50,000 well-trained Germans were able to defeat two million conscripted Frenchmen.

Admittedly, anti-interventionists conceded, the United States Army needed hundreds of thousands of skilled mechanics, pilots, and technicians. Conscription, however, merely provided millions of raw recruits with a year's training in bayonet practice, military drills, and manual of arms exercises. As Senator Edwin Johnson (Dem.-Colo.) commented, "Minutemen went out of style with the flintlock musket."

Weaknesses in training and equipment were emphasized. If "you put two million men in training to use a gun," remarked Congressman Usher Burdick (Rep.-N. D.), you "will do just about as much good as to attempt to grow feathers on a fish." Publisher Robert R. McCormick mourned the lack of a single heavy tank. Congressman Harold Knutson (Rep.-Minn.) jested, "If the additional million were called to the colors under this legislation, would it not place a considerable strain on our supply of broomsticks?"

Roosevelt's critics also found the proposal undemocratic. Senator Arthur Capper (Rep.-Kan.) claimed it would "Prussianize the young men of America." To Norman Thomas, conscription meant "Hitlerism in the name of defending democracy." Congressman U. S. Guyer (Rep.-Kan.) called it a "war slave plan." Wheeler warned, "If you pass this bill, you slit the throat of the last democracy still living; you accord to Hitler his greatest and cheapest victory to date." Taft spelled out why he saw the legislation as patently unfair. (*See Document No. 13.*)

To the anti-interventionists, voluntary enlistment remained the responsible alternative. So far, they argued, the volunteer system was working well. Early in August, Capper found every quota of the army filled. Fish claimed that with 400,000 already in the National Guard and 375,000 expected in the Regular Army and reserves, the United States already possessed close to 800,000 forces. If this number could not defeat 50,000 foreign troops, "then we better give up anyway."

General Marshall challenged all such figures. If any enemy attacked, he claimed, at least 1.2 million defending troops would be needed, and if danger threatened the entire Hemisphere, the United States might require over four million men. Moreover, an army that had to depend solely on either one-year volunteers or conscripts would soon cease to have a trained nucleus. *Time* magazine took the argument even further. Volunteer recruiting, it conceded, could maintain a standing army so long as the United States remained at peace. But in wartime a draft was the only way of assuring a reserve of prepared manpower.

By mid-August the Gallup poll had indicated 70 percent in favor of the draft. On September 16, conscription legislation—having passed both houses—was signed by President Roosevelt. The final bill involved some modification of the Burke-Wadsworth proposal. Only those between ages twenty-one and thirty-six were required to register. General Marshall was now authorized to call upon 900,000 men annually. Those inducted would serve in the armed forces for twelve months, then enter the reserves. They could not, however, be stationed outside the United States and its territories. Even then, the task of creating a mass army was not easy. Many a draftee had to use a broomstick instead of a rifle, the very fear of Representative Knutson.

Politics—But Not as Usual. On June 20, at the very time the Burke-Wadsworth bill was being introduced, Roosevelt announced two crucial appointments to his cabinet. First, the seventy-two-year-old Henry L. Stimson, a staunch Republican, would head the War Department. He had been secretary of war once before, from 1911 to 1913 under President William Howard Taft, and secretary of state under Hoover. An ardent interventionist, Stimson had publicly endorsed "universal compulsory training and service," the immediate repeal of the Neutrality Act, and the opening of all U.S. ports to British and French ships needing repairs. Calling for a marked acceleration of aircraft shipments to the Allies, he mentioned the possibility of American ships convoying such armaments.

Second, FDR chose Frank Knox, publisher of the *Chicago Daily News*, to head the Navy Department. Knox, who was sixty-six years old, had been Republican vice-presidential candidate just four years previously. Knox wanted an army of a million men and the largest air force in the world. He would put "at the disposal of the British all the munitions and supplies needed to keep the battle going." Given the age, party affiliation, and lack of immediate experience of the two appointees, it was obvious that the president was seeking to create some bipartisan support in light of an imminent presidential race. In this he was most successful, historian Robert A. Divine (*Foreign Policy and U.S. Presidential Elections, 1940–1960* [1974]) calling the move "a political triumph."

Anti-interventionists were furious. Hugh Johnson found the appointments of "poisonous significance," as both men were "ardent tom-tom beaters for war." To Boake Carter, himself the son of a British diplomat and educated at Cambridge, they were both "poor Americans." Senator Vandenberg claimed that under Stimson's open-port recommendation, the recent battle of Oran could have been fought in New York harbor. (In the battle of Mers-el-Kebir at Oran in North Africa, which took place on July 3, the British navy had bombarded the defeated French fleet to keep it from falling into Nazi hands.)

Yet the interventionists easily won the battle. On July 9, the Senate confirmed Stimson 56 to 28. A day later Knox received even greater support, the vote being 66 to 16. The Republican national chairman, John Hamilton, promptly expelled Stimson and Knox from the party.

The Destroyer-Bases Deal. Many anti-interventionists were even more alarmed, when on September 3 the president, acting by executive agreement, agreed to transfer fifty overage destroyers to the British. In exchange, the United States would receive the right to take ninety-nine-year leases on naval and air bases in Newfoundland, Bermuda, the Bahamas, Jamaica, St. Lucia, Trinidad, Antigua, and British Guinea. In retrospect, neither the bases nor the destroyers played a major role in the war. Yet, diplomatically, the agreement marked a major step toward intervention.

As with the draft, several anti-interventionists endorsed the move. Colonel McCormick praised the administration for turning the Caribbean into "an American lake." The *New York Daily News* found it the greatest achievement of the Roosevelt administration to date.

Nevertheless, far more anti-interventionists were outraged. Flynn called for Roosevelt's impeachment. To Hearst, the agreement was an act of aggression, to Nye and Fish an act of war. The *St. Louis Post-Dispatch*, at times pro-New Deal, called the president "America's first dictator." (*See Document No. 14.*) Edward S. Corwin, a leading constitutional scholar at Princeton, said the move was "an endorsement of unrestrained autocracy in the field of foreign relations."

Besides, some FDR critics claimed, the United States might still need the ships. Senator Henry Cabot Lodge (Rep.-Mass.) saw no such thing as "a surplus of weapons." Hugh Johnson queried with characteristic wryness: if the United States destroyers were so obsolete, why did the British claim that the life of its navy depended on them?

Alternatives were offered. Fish proposed that the United States cancel Britain's long-standing war debt in return for total ownership of all off-shore islands, a proposal that had often been made by extreme "isolationists." The arch-rightist monthly digest *Scribner's Commentator* suggested the mortgaging of British hemispheric possessions for a ten-billion-dollar loan. Dorothy Detzer, national secretary of the U.S. WIL, claimed the United States should first purchase the islands, then put them under a Pan-American flag. Public opinion polls, however, indicated widespread support for the president.

The Campaign of 1940. In 1940 there was to be a presidential election. As widespread dissatisfaction existed with a stagnant economy and bottlenecks in defense, the Republicans hoped to capture both the White House and Congress. Until the very eve of the party convention, all the major presidential hopefuls were strong anti-interventionists. Particularly militant on the issue was Senator Taft, the favorite of the state organizations and second in the polls. Even as the British were being driven to the shores of northern France, he was telling voters, "This is not the time for the people to be wholly absorbed in foreign quarrels."

Senator Vandenberg was far more militant on the New Deal than Taft, but had replaced the deceased Borah as the Grand Old Party's leading anti-interventionist. The Michigan senator could not launch any boom. By the time the party convention met, he was little more than a dark horse.

It was, however, Thomas E. Dewey, New York City's crime-busting district attorney, who was endorsed by anti-interventionist newspapers possessing a huge circulation, among them the *New York Daily News*, the *Chicago Tribune*, and William Randolph Hearst's *San Francisco Examiner*. Dewey won major primaries in Wisconsin and Nebraska and led a Gallup poll in March with 43 percent, twice the backing of the next contender. As late as March, Dewey was telling audiences that the United States must "keep its hands wholly out of the European war." By the time the convention met in mid-June, Dewey had moderated his position but still opposed sending American warships to aid the British. Other candidates wanted at best limited aid overseas.

The Republicans, however, held their convention just as France had signed the armistice with Hitler. The party quickly settled on Wendell Willkie, a public utilities magnate who until recently had been a Democrat. Willkie's moderate interventionism—favoring sending munitions but not troops—was a major factor in his nomination. He was the first modern "media candidate," being strongly backed by such staunchly pro-Allied publishers as Henry R. Luce (Time-Life), John and Gardner Cowles (*Des Moines Register* and *Look* magazine), and Helen and Ogden Reid (*New York Herald Tribune*).

On the Democratic side, there was brief talk about running Senator Wheeler, a man whom CIO president John L. Lewis strongly supported. Once, however, Roosevelt permitted himself to be open to a "draft," his nomination was a foregone conclusion.

Both Democratic and Republican planks pledged themselves to hemispheric defense, aid to Britain, and keeping all troops at home. Each candidate supported conscription, which the bulk of Republicans in Congress opposed and their Democratic counterparts favored.

Anti-interventionists attacked FDR far more than Willkie. In his book *Country Squire in the White House* (1940), John T. Flynn accused Roosevelt of becoming "the recognized leader of the war party" in order to "take the minds of the people off the failure to solve our own problems"—problems that included some eleven million unemployed, a mounting public debt, and the paralysis of private investment. The president, he said, was likely soon to engage in a "military adventure." Charles A. Lindbergh's opposition was more couched, the aviator saying that the nation needed "leaders whose promises we can trust, who know where they are taking us, and who can tell us where they are going."

During the campaign, FDR and Willkie sought to outbid each other in promises to avoid war. Willkie attacked the destroyer-bases deal, saying that if Roosevelt were reelected, "he may trade away the Philippines without consulting Congress." In attacking FDR directly, he told a Chicago rally, "If his promise to keep our boys out of foreign wars is no better than his promise to balance the budget, they're almost on the transports!" Roosevelt was quick to respond. On October 30, while in Boston, he made a statement that would later haunt him: "I have said this before, but I shall say it again and again and again: Your boys are not going to be sent into any foreign wars."

On November 5, the president was reelected. He garnered over 27.3 million votes, almost 5 million more than Willkie. In the electoral college, the tally was 449 to 82. Without doubt, the international situation was a major factor in FDR's victory, and here the fall of France played a particularly prominent role. The Democrats kept control of the Congress. Republicans were soon blaming Willkie for not being more critical of intervention while, once the campaign was over, Willkie quickly rallied behind Roosevelt's foreign policy. Anti-interventionists could take comfort in only one fact: many outspoken opponents of FDR's foreign policy were reelected, including Vandenberg, Wheeler, Fish, Hiram Johnson, and Senator Robert M. La Follette, Jr. (Prog.-Wis.)

Anti-interventionists Organize. In May 1940, the interventionists had established another pressure group, this one even better organized and financed than the one formed in October 1939 to revise the Neutrality Act. It was again headed by editor William Allen White, who was national chairman. Clark Eichelberger, national director of the League of Nations Association, was executive director. The Committee to Defend America by Aiding the Allies (CDAAA), as it was named, worked in tandem with the Roosevelt administration. Dedicated to increasing aid to the British, the CDAAA vigorously endorsed the destroyer-bases deal though it remained neutral on conscription. By late summer, more militant voices within the CDAAA, who in April 1941 formed the Fight for Freedom Committee, were making more radical proposals: the massive shipments of American weapons to Britain, including pursuit planes, tanks, the top secret Norden bombsight, high-speed torpedo craft (called mosquito boats), and four-engine bombers (called Flying Fortresses).

It was such proposals that led Roosevelt critics to establish their own action group, first called the Emergency Committee to Defend America First but in late August renamed the America First Committee (AFC).

The AFC remained in existence until Germany declared war on the United States, formally disbanding only on December 11, 1941.

For an extremely brief period, the AFC had a rival. In mid-December 1940 Verne Marshall, editor of the *Cedar Rapids* (Iowa) *Gazette*, established a similar organization, the No Foreign War Committee. The leader's mercurial personality, however, soon lead to its demise.

The concept of an AFC had originated late in the spring of 1940. Yale law student R. Douglas Stuart, Jr. launched a drive to organize college students into a nationwide anti-interventionist organization. Among the petition's four drafters were Gerald R. Ford, Jr. and Potter Stewart, later respectively president of the United States and associate justice on the United States Supreme Court. In toto the document read:

We believe that the United States must now concentrate all its energies upon building a strong defense for this hemisphere.

We believe that today our American democracy can only be preserved by keeping out of the war abroad.

We oppose any increase in supplies to England beyond the limitations of cash and carry in the belief that it would imperil American strength and lead to active American intervention in Europe.

We demand Congress refrain from war, even if England is on the verge of defeat.

The law students soon enlarged their focus, seeking supporters in all areas of national life. General Robert E. Wood, sixty-one-year-old board chairman of Sears, Roebuck, volunteered to lead a national organization and immediately became its acting chairman. As in the original declaration of the Yale students, the AFC offered a four-point program:

1. The United States must build an impregnable defense for America.
2. No foreign power, nor group of powers, can successfully attack a *prepared* America.
3. American democracy can be preserved only by keeping out of the European war.
4. "Aid short of war" weakens national defense at home and threatens to involve America in war abroad.

On September 5 Hugh Johnson officially led off the committee with a nationwide radio broadcast. (*See Document No. 15.*)

Prominent supporters included retired diplomat William R. Castle, Hoover's undersecretary of state; Chicago attorney Clay Judson, who had headed his city's Council of Foreign Relations; Kathryn Lewis, who undoubtedly represented her father John L. Lewis, by far the nation's most powerful labor leader; Al Williams, a Scripps-Howard columnist and leading advocate of air power; Chicago investor Sterling Morton, long a staunch conservative; and New York advertising executive Chester Bowles. John T. Flynn directed the New York chapter, a particularly activist unit holding rallies on city street corners. Stuart took a leave of absence from Yale, first becoming national director, then executive secretary. Gerald Ford, who was working his way through law school as an assistant football coach for Yale, soon quit the movement on the grounds that interventionist alumni might get him fired. Yet another personal friend of Stuart's, young John F. Kennedy, contributed a hundred dollars to the organization, writing, "What you are doing is vital."

Colonel McCormick and Captain Patterson, publishers respectively of the *Chicago Tribune* and the *New York Daily News*, helped bankroll the committee as did Chicago textile manufacturer William H. Regnery, Chicago investment banker Harold R. Stuart, and New York chemical manufacturer H. Smith Richardson. For the anti-interventionists, such backing was vital, because almost immediately the AFC was involved in the fight of its life, a struggle centering around something known as "lend-lease."

CHAPTER 5

ATLANTIC PREPARATIONS

Britain's Predicament. By the beginning of winter, Hitler's strength had grown. Germany's allies now included Hungary and a truncated Romania, the latter occupied by *Wehrmacht* troops. By October 1940 Hitler realized that *Luftwaffe* bombers were not winning the Battle of Britain; hence he turned his attention to England's oceanic lifeline, hoping that U-boats might starve the British into submission. Already the island nation was experiencing heavy shipping losses—over 400,000 tons that very October.

Moreover, British dollar reserves were running low, a situation that threatened Britain's capacity to purchase American supplies. Yet the 1939 neutrality law, centering on cash-and-carry, banned extension of U.S. credit while the 1934 Johnson Act, sponsored by arch-isolationist Senator Hiram Johnson, prohibited private loans to countries that had defaulted on World War I debts to the American government or its citizens.

On December 7, 1940, Winston Churchill, the British prime minister, warned Roosevelt that Britain would soon lack the cash to buy the American weapons it so desperately needed. America's own future was at stake, he warned, claiming that the safety of the United States was linked to the survival of the British Commonwealth. Conversely, there was a warning: if the unoccupied part of France, popularly known as the Vichy government, went over to Hitler and if France's remaining navy were to join the Axis, control of West Africa would pass into its hands. Then, once the Germans seized Dakar, South America would become vulnerable.

Roosevelt's Response: The Lend-Lease Bill. In responding to Churchill's plea, the president refused to be stymied by existing legislation. At a press conference held on December 17, FDR announced that he would not tamper with either the 1939 Neutrality Act or the Johnson Act. Rather he would try something "brand new," a mechanism whereby the United States could take over British orders, then "lease or sell" what it thought the British needed. He said he would

39

leave "out the dollar sign in the form of a debt" and substitute "a gentleman's agreement to repay in kind."

Nine days later, FDR gave one of his "fireside chats," in which he called Great Britain and the British Empire "the spearhead of resistance to world conquest." If Britain "goes down," he declared, "the Axis powers will control the continents of Europe, Asia, Africa, Australasia, and the high seas and they will be in a position to bring enormous military and naval resources against this hemisphere." Even more than in May, Roosevelt stressed danger from the air. Bombers, he maintained, could fly from Dakar to Brazil in five hours, and could travel from the British Isles to New England without refueling. Rather than permit the United States to live "at the point of a gun," he announced that the nation would be "the great arsenal of democracy" and that all possible aid would reach Britain. Taking a swipe at the anti-interventionists, he warned against "American citizens, many of them in high places," who—usually unwittingly—were "aiding and abetting" the work of destructive foreign agents.

On January 6, 1941, the president gave his State-of-the-Union address to Congress. In advancing his plan, he spoke of a "world founded on four essential freedoms"—freedom of speech and expression, freedom of worship, freedom from want, and freedom from fear. Denying that such goals were utopian, he claimed that they were "attainable in our own time and generation."

Four days later the bill was introduced to Congress. Given the innocent title lend-lease and deliberately labeled H. R. 1776, its terms were nothing if not sweeping. The president could provide military articles and information to any country "whose defense the President deems vital to the defense of the United States." He had complete discretion concerning terms for transfer. If he so desired, the terms "defense article" and "defense information" could permit virtually anything to fall under one of the two categories, military secrets included. *Newsweek* was not inaccurate when it said that Roosevelt would be given permission to lend "anything from a trench shovel to a battle ship." No limits were set on quantity of weapons loaned, sums to be allocated. The president could release military secrets and set aside international law. Friendly belligerents could use American ports.

Even the interventionist press could only marvel. *Time* found it unique, declaring that under its terms, "powers would go to Franklin Roosevelt such as no American has ever before asked for." Similarly

Newsweek noted that "its sweeping language entrusted the nation's future to Franklin D. Roosevelt more completely than it had ever been entrusted to George Washington or Abraham Lincoln." "Millions of Americans," it continued, "are still gaping."

Anti-interventionists Balk. Of course, to anti-interventionists, the bill was dynamite. Some comments were apocalyptic. The legislation sought "the enslavement of free Americans." It abrogated the Declaration of Independence. It put "the very fate of our democratic government at stake." The *Christian Century* called it "the most un-American proposal which the American people have ever had seriously to consider."

When it came to serious criticism, the matter of presidential powers was foremost. To historian Charles A. Beard, the bill authorized Roosevelt himself to "wage undeclared wars for anybody anywhere in the world, until the affairs of the world suit his policies, not to mention the dissipation of U.S. strength." (*See Document No. 16.*) Other scholars concurred. To historian Howard K. Beale, "the very fate of our democratic government" was at stake. John Bassett Moore, the first American justice ever to sit on the World Court, said, "the question is whether we shall have a government of law or a government of men."

The anti-interventionists advanced a second argument, namely that lend-lease would weaken American defenses. General Hanford Mac-Nider, AFC vice chairman and former U.S. minister to Canada, called it "the triple-threat bill—lease, lend, and lose America's defenses." Charles A. Lindbergh found the U.S. air force more stripped than ever. Al Williams denied that the United States possessed a single modern plane with the needed number of guns. Even an obsolete plane, he said, was "actually worth its weight in gold, to train man power for the air power we need so critically today." The category "defense article," so Wheeler claimed, embraced "all articles from battleships to bath powders, from bombers to the billions of gold buried in old Kentucky, from cannon to Willkie buttons. . . . on the sinister side they include crutches and artificial limbs and books in Braille type and identification tags and coffins and crosses for the countless future victims of our folly."

Third, anti-interventionists found the economic consequences indeed staggering. A prominent lumber merchant called it "The Nation's Bankrupting Act of 1941." The bill, said the AFC, fostered inflation, unemployment, and loss of consumer income.

Fourth, certain critics found the bill warlike. To Taft, the president, "sitting behind the scenes," "can pull the strings which fire the guns, and drop the bombs on armed forces and helpless civilians alike." Professor Borchard asserted that one could not "authorize the commission of flagrant acts of war, and leave the country under the impression that you are not engaging in war."

Some anti-interventionists questioned British claims of impoverishment, declaring that Britain had several billion dollars' worth of securities in the United States. Others feared that the bill made U.S. convoys inevitable, and indeed claimed that the bill gave the administration the requisite authority. Despite the president's disclaimers, historian Warren Kimball (*The Most Unsordid Act: Lend-Lease, 1939–1941* [1969]) notes that Roosevelt had indeed been thinking about American convoying, in fact about a diplomatic break with the Axis.

Proposed Alternatives. Many anti-interventionists did not endorse cutting off all aid to Britain. Rather they preferred a straight loan, even an outright grant. Taft and Fish both made such proposals. Hoover wanted to give Britain all the defense items it needed, plus some two or three billion dollars to buy other materials. Then, he said, let them fight the war as they see fit. The AFC's General Wood suggested selling spare U.S. ships to Britain and providing long-term credits for food and war supplies.

Both the administration and its critics, however, saw just what was behind such proposals. If the United States merely made loans or gave money, its stake in the war would be relatively limited. The Lend-Lease bill, on the other hand, grafted the American economy to the British war effort. It involved the distinct possibility that the United States might be called upon to see the goods delivered safely. The ultimate question: Was the United States willing to see the matter through? This really was the issue at stake.

Results of the Bill's Passage. Obviously congressional debate was sharp, but the measure never lacked the needed votes. In the House it carried 260–165, the Senate 60–31, and on March 11, 1941, the president signed the bill. The polls indicated popular approval: on February 14 Gallup showed 58 percent totally in favor and 14 percent giving qualified support.

In conclusion, what can be said about the Lend-Lease Act? As the British historian David Reynolds (*The Creation of the Anglo-American Alliance, 1937–41* [1981]) notes, at first lend-lease aid was quite limited. Only later did the British and its Commonwealth nations receive some $31 billion in supplies, the Soviet Union $11 billion. Furthermore, contrary to the accusations of many anti-interventionists, there were no gifts involved. Supplies were not free. Repayment was simply postponed, not waived. Later administration discussions show that the "consideration" would not be in money or even in kind, but would lie in a commitment to America's conception of the postwar world economy, one that would force the British to give up their whole economic preference system.

The bill was of crucial importance, however, because it marked the forging of an irrevocable Anglo-American alliance. The United States now assumed responsibility for Britain's long-term purchases in America, something that relieved the British government of an impossible burden. Roosevelt was staking the fate of his entire nation on Britain's chances for survival.

Initial Convoys. At the very time that lend-lease was being passed, the war was going badly for the British. German Afrika Korps commander Erwin Rommel had seized Libya and was threatening Egypt. Greece and Crete had fallen to Hitler's troops. By March, Nazi sinkings of British craft totaled over half a million tons per month, roughly a quarter of the British fleet. In fact, on a single night early in April, the Germans sank ten ships in a British convoy of twenty-two. U.S. chief of naval operations, Admiral Harold R. Stark, called the situation "hopeless, except as we take strong measures to save it." There seemed only one answer—convoys by the United States itself, for the Royal Navy could not spare the needed destroyers and cruisers. On April 8, however, opinion polls showed that the public opposed escorting by 50 to 41 percent.

On April 18, 1941, Roosevelt established a "neutrality patrol" in the western Atlantic, though he lacked the ships to make it effective. Its mission: to "observe and report" belligerent movements and keep war from "our front doors." (The U.S. Navy had sought full-scale escort.) The patrol would flash the location of German U-boats, thereby alerting British merchantmen to veer away while inviting British cruisers and destroyers to attack. What was called the U.S. "neutrality" or "security" zone, originally sixty degrees west, would now reach twenty-six degrees longitude west, hence encompassing all Greenland plus the Azores. As this vast expanse overlapped a German combat zone proclaimed on March 25, an eventual clash was assured.

The American ships and planes lacked the authority to attack. Hence FDR insisted that the operation was indeed a *patrol*, and thereby limited to scouting, and not an *escort*, with its heightened risk of combat. Such semantic juggling could not hide the severe risks involved.

Anti-interventionists were most apprehensive. Early in April Senator Tobey introduced a resolution to prohibit U.S. escorts for British ships. Though backed by the AFC, within a month it died in committee. Taft saw convoys as a deliberate effort to entice the United States into war. (*See Document No. 17.*) Anti-interventionists questioned British claims of losses and accused the British shipping industry of still competing with U.S. traffic and goods. They denounced a presidential decree of April 4 that permitted American merchant vessels to carry goods to Aden, a British port close to the Suez Canal, and thereby supply British forces in Egypt and the Middle East.

Greenland. Not only was Roosevelt extending a security zone far into the Atlantic, but on April 9, he signed a major agreement with the Danish government, one that permitted the United States to occupy Greenland. The Danish minister in Washington lacked any authority to make such a deal, and the Nazi-dominated government at home immediately disavowed the arrangement. Yet Greenland's strategic value was simply too vital to be passed up. In enemy hands, warned Assistant Secretary of State Adolf A. Berle, Jr., planes from Greenland could strike at New York. In friendly hands, however, the island expedited the delivery of short-range aircraft to Britain.

On this issue, anti-interventionists were split. For at least a year, some Roosevelt critics had stressed the value of Greenland's strategic sites and its possession of such minerals as cryolite, valuable in aluminum refining. Hence Congressman Fish, the *New York Daily News*, and the *Chicago Tribune* had endorsed U.S. control. Even Charles A. Lindbergh thought minor U.S. bases might be placed there, though he denied that Greenland was a good launching site for an enemy invasion.

Other anti-interventionists, however, were alarmed. Congressman

George Bender (Rep.-Ohio) warned that the United States would be patrolling an area 2,600 miles from the American mainland. The *Christian Century* described Greenland as "a vast territory covered with perpetual ice"; it accused Roosevelt of "betraying" the United States into war over useless land.

Iceland. On July 7, a brigade of nearly four thousand U.S. Marines arrived in Iceland in order to relieve British and Canadian troops stationed there. Iceland was a sovereign state in personal union with then-occupied Denmark, but since May 1940 it had been occupied by Britain. The action, claimed FDR after the fact, was a preventive one. In his message to Congress and the nation, Roosevelt claimed that German occupation of that strategic island would lead to hostile naval and air bases menacing Greenland, thereby threatening shipping in the North Atlantic and interrupting the steady flow of munitions to Britain. Conversely, in friendly hands, Iceland provided indispensable refueling bases for convoys and controlled the Denmark Strait, a passage between Greenland and Iceland where German ships had been particularly active. Within two weeks, the U.S. Navy was escorting American and Icelandic ships to its new outpost, the very development feared by foes of lend-lease. Sixty-one percent of Gallup poll respondents endorsed the president's message; only 20 percent were definitely opposed.

Most anti-interventionists, however, were furious. Only the *New York Daily News* was willing to give the administration the benefit of the doubt, declaring it was willing to take the navy's word that Iceland was a genuine strategic outpost. For many FDR critics, the move was an act of war. Indeed the editorial headline in the *Christian Century* read: "The President Enters the War." Hanson Baldwin commented, "Iceland cannot be guarded indefinitely without shooting." Furthermore, so some anti-interventionists claimed, the president had no authority to order troops there: "The mere fact that power may be usurped is no evidence of legal right." Professor Corwin opposed declaring war on Germany if the Nazis attacked Iceland, claiming that the venture had been made without due preparation and without consulting Congress. Flynn remarked, "If the President, without the consent of Congress, can occupy Iceland, he can occupy Syria or Ethiopia." Still other anti-interventionists found the territory of no strategic value. To editor Waldrop, four-fifths of Iceland was uninhabitable. It lacked a harbor, was too remote to build airstrips, and produced nothing but "hay, geysers, and herring."

Yet, between the time that U.S. troops were sent to Iceland and Greenland, the entire nature of the war had changed, thanks to a campaign that Hitler labeled Operation Barbarossa.

CHAPTER 6

A DIFFERENT FRONT

Invasion of Russia. On the night of June 21, 1941, Hitler launched the greatest onslaught in the history of warfare. Aligning 3.2 million men and 148 divisions ranged over a thousand mile frontier, he invaded the Soviet Union.

Once the invasion took place, Roosevelt acted quickly, unfreezing some $39 million of Russian funds and directing the release of machine tools for Moscow. He refrained from invoking the Neutrality Act, thus enabling American ships to carry munitions to any port. At the end of July 1941, the president sent his leading adviser, Harry Hopkins, to Moscow, there to discern whether the Soviets were capable of resisting the German onslaught. If the Russians were strong enough, American military aid would be shipped.

The Soviet Union: An Object of Wariness. Ever since the war had broken out in Europe, anti-interventionists on all points on the political spectrum shared one major fear: that the sheer continuation of the war would result in the geographical expansion of the Soviet Union and with it the ideology of communism. The Russians were simply biding their time, to use Taft's metaphor "sitting on the sidelines," while the other major powers destroyed themselves. Once Europe was decimated, Red revolution would spread from the Urals to the Rhine, perhaps even touching lands as disparate as Persia, India, Britain—and the United States.

Not surprisingly, those anti-interventionists who were conservatives quickly expressed their apprehension. Once the belligerents were "bled white," said Fish in the fall of 1939, "the Communist vulture will sweep down on the bloody remains of Europe." D. Worth Clark even envisioned France and England in Stalin's arms. Congressman Dondero saw the Russian dictator's eyes on China and the Philippines. In March 1940 one editorial headline in the *Chicago Tribune* read: "The Winner, Red Josef." That October, General Wood predicted that another year of war would result in "communism in all Europe" and "a species of national socialism in England." In fact "it probably means the end of capitalism all over the world."

Yet those anti-interventionists who were liberals or on the democratic left were equally apprehensive. In October 1939 the *New York Daily News*, a pro-New Deal paper, thought Russia aspired to British India; indeed the United States might end up "the only non-Communist nation left in the world." Norman Thomas wrote FDR directly, warning that a victorious Stalin, having watched his rivals destroy themselves, might be able to "establish a kind of world hegemony." Another Socialist, editor Oscar Ameringer, went so far as to say that "Hitler's Germany is now a dependency of Soviet Russia."

Journalist Freda Utley took the anti-Soviet stance to its most extreme. A British subject who would soon become an American citizen, she had lost her husband in the Gulag, though she did not know yet that he was already dead. Writing in July 1940, she went so far as to say: "The Russian brand of national socialism is even more oppressive, and far more destructive of life and material prosperity, than the German. So that absorption by the U.S.S.R. is even more feared than Nazi domination by the little states close to Russia."

Like Utley, many anti-interventionists on the right and left saved their most negative invective not for Germany and Hitler but for the Soviet Union and Stalin. Air columnist Al Williams called the Soviet Union "the bloodiest sponsor of mass murder in the pages of history." Hiram Johnson said of Russia's dictator, "The greatest blood-letting that was ever committed on this earth occurred through him." The *Chicago Tribune* called Stalin "the man responsible for more human misery than any since the Mongolian invasions." To the *New York Daily News*, Stalin was "even more of a beast" than Hitler. Helicopter manufacturer Igor Sikorsky, himself Russian-born and educated, accused the Soviets of destroying between twenty-five and forty million lives. Indeed 200,000 people died just in building a canal from the Baltic to the White Sea.

Anti-interventionists Fight U.S. Aid. When, in June 1941, Hitler's force launched his attack, most anti-interventionists strongly opposed American aid to the defenders. One of the most extreme comments came from Charles A. Lindbergh, who said early in July, "I would a hundred times rather see my country ally herself with England, or even with Germany with all her faults, than the cruelty, the Godlessness, and the barbarism that exists in Soviet Russia."

On moral grounds alone, it was argued, the Soviets did not deserve aid. Indeed, to give them military assistance simply made a travesty of any war against totalitarian dictatorship. Intervention now, said Hoover, would be a "gargantuan jest." To Fish, the "lend-lease" bill was being transformed into a "Lenin-lease" bill. Taft claimed that the slogan "Bundles for Britain," also the title of a popular charity, would be followed by "Packages for Petrograd." Sterling Morton offered a variation, "Mufflers for Moscow."

One should not choose between evils, the anti-interventionists maintained; one should simply stay out of the fracas. R. Douglas Stuart, Jr., the AFC's executive secretary, wrote Hoover on June 28, 1941 (from manuscripts of the AFC [Box 3] at the Hoover Institution Library):

The outbreak of war between Russia and Germany has had a notable influence on public opinion. People realize there is no choice for us. If Germany wins, Russia will go Fascist. If Russia wins, Germany will go Communist. The American people are not anxious to fight to make the world safe for communism.

Particularly galling was Roosevelt's claim that the Soviet Union enjoyed freedom of worship. In his effort to secure backing for his policy of aiding the Soviets, the president told a press conference in late September that the 1936 Soviet constitution protected the free exercise of religion.

Anti-interventionists were quick to respond. *Uncensored* accused Roosevelt of showing "symptoms of juridical cretinism." Speaking of Stalin, it said: "To demonstrate his sincerity, he could order every Muscovite into Red Square to take communion at Lenin's tomb." Fish suggested that Roosevelt baptize Stalin in the White House swimming pool.

To some anti-interventionists, the quick German advance conveyed no alarm. The AFC prepared a memo claiming that Hitler's conquest of Russia would add little to Germany's wealth. (*See Document No. 18.*) Conversely Unitarian pacifist John Haynes Holmes feared what a victorious Soviet Union would do. (*See Document No. 19.*) Occasionally an anti-interventionist saw a cold war in the offing. Asked the *Saturday Evening Post*, "Having saved the world from Nazism, should we not be morally obligated to go on and save it from Bolshevism?"

Congress Votes Aid to the Soviets. When Hopkins reported affirmatively on his fact-finding mission, Roosevelt, acting on Septem-

ber 18, included aid to the Soviets in a supplementary lend-lease appropriations bill of six billion dollars. Opponents proposed an amendment
that excluded the Russians, but it was voted down by both houses.

The polls showed wide support for the president's Russian policy. For
example, *Fortune* magazine, canvassing the public in October, found
51.4 percent of the respondents saying the United States should work
alongside the Russians. An additional 21.9 percent hoped the Soviets
would be treated as full partners. Only 13.5 percent took the position
held by most anti-interventionists: the United States should cut off all
aid to the Russians.

Despite the intensity of the debate over Russia, American lend-lease
probably had little initial impact on the battle front. Delivery of goods
was always difficult, indeed dangerous. Roosevelt and Hopkins themselves conceded that such aid was more a matter of American good faith
than of immediate value to the Soviet war effort. As far as the impending winter of 1941–42 went, they realized that U.S. supplies would play
a negligible part in the ongoing battle for Moscow. In fact, little could
arrive until after that military outcome had already been decided.

Extending the Term of Military Service. The Selective
Service Act of 1940 had limited the time of service for draftees to
twelve months. Furthermore, it prohibited draftees from serving outside the Western Hemisphere. By 1941, however, General Marshall saw
crisis ahead. Testifying before the Senate Military Affairs Committee
on July 17, he urged Congress to extend indefinitely the terms of draftees, National Guardsmen, and reserve officers. Otherwise, he continued, "our present trained forces will largely melt away." He soon noted
certain potential dangers—the Axis conquest of Alaska, Nazi uprisings
in Bolivia, Brazil, and Colombia—and pointed to war clouds gathering
in the Far East. A few days after Marshall made his report, the War
Department requested that the hemispheric restrictions be lifted.

In a special message sent to Congress on July 21, Roosevelt claimed
that the peril was "infinitely greater" than it had been a year before.
Each German conquest brought Nazi domination that much closer to
the Western Hemisphere. "Within two months," he said, "disintegra-
tion, which would follow failure to take Congressional action, will com-
mence in the armies of the United States." He called for Congress to
"acknowledge" a national emergency, something that would thereby
give the president authority to hold soldiers "for the duration."

The public was far from receptive, as shown by a Gallup poll of July 29 indicating that only 51 percent favored eliminating the one-year limit. In bargaining with congressional leaders, Roosevelt was forced to retain the ban on serving outside the hemisphere, though he did manage to secure endorsement for lifting the one-year restriction. Furthermore, FDR's original request that Congress declare a national emergency was dropped.

Anti-interventionist Opposition. Again, the anti-interventionists balked. Some found the existing army sufficiently strong. Before the draft was passed in 1940, they claimed, the United States had less than 300,000 in actual service. If one currently added 1.5 million reservists to National Guardsmen, reserve officers, and regular troops, the U.S. Army contained close to four and a half million men. Congressman Dewey Short (Rep.-Mo.) suggested that just as enlistments were staggered over all twelve months, so too could demobilization. The *Chicago Tribune* claimed that a volunteer force of less than 500,000, if properly armed and trained, could ably defend the country.

Furthermore, the administration was accused of breaking faith with the draftees. To the *New York Daily News*, it was playing "a dirty trick." Miserable training conditions only compounded the breach of faith. Anti-interventionists pointed to primitive facilities in the army camps, marked salary inequities between soldiers and factory workers, and the misuse of troops by permitting them to be used as strike-breakers. Commenting on the lack of proper training equipment, Bennett Champ Clark noted maneuvers in which an ordinary truck bore the sign: "This is a tank." Administration critics noted that other countries, ranging from Canada to Germany, trained their recruits in much less time.

Anti-interventionists challenged Roosevelt's claim that the United States was more imperiled in 1941 than in 1940. The Germans, they noted, had so far lost a million men in the Russian campaign, in addition to huge quantities of munitions, bombers, tanks, and airplanes. In late July the *Christian Century* asked rhetorically "Is the Nation in Peril?" and answered with a resounding no. Queried Senator Alva Adams, "Can we imagine Germany, surrounded by hostile peoples whom she has overrun, with her hands more than filled in meeting Russia, and with the British fleet on the other side, undertaking to invade the United States?" Suppose, said Taft, the Germans did succeed in conquering Russia. A considerable part of it would be tied down in occupation duties throughout Europe.

Allied successes on the battlefield were marked. Within a year, FDR critics stressed, Britain had conquered Italian East Africa, Ethiopia, and French Syria. In the words of Senator Alexander Wiley (Rep.-Wis.), it was "out-Coventrying, on Germany's soil, the German Luftwaffe's bombardment of Coventry." The AFC pointed to a number of factors: Hitler's indefinite postponement of invading Britain, Germany engaged in fighting its strongest opponent on the European continent, a fall in British sea losses during the summer, and a much stronger British air defense.

Nor was the Far East neglected. Bender stressed that China was holding out. Singapore and the Netherlands East Indies, said Senator Wiley, were equipped and garrisoned. Moreover, despite Japan's recent move into Indochina, the island empire had been weakened both financially and in the matter of manpower. Conversely, the United States had strengthened its navy, fortified its island possessions, and cut off fuel oil to Japan.

By the same token, the United States' own defenses appeared much improved. Wheeler denied he could find a single U.S. naval officer who claimed that the German navy outnumbered the American one. Addressing himself to the submarine issue, the Montana senator denied that German craft were built for distance; rather they were constructed for action around the Baltic and along the Atlantic coast. Conversely, U.S. subs were constructed for long-range service. Furthermore, as Wiley noted, the new American bases had turned the Caribbean into "an American lake."

General Marshall's desire to lift the ban on service overseas met with much anxiety. A new American Expeditionary Force might well be in the making. Vandenberg accused the army chief of staff of seeking "an unlimited army, with unlimited tenure of service, and with the authority to send it anywhere on earth." Congressman Daniel A. Reed (Rep.-N.Y.) declared, "If this is an army for an expedition abroad, then we should be beginning now to lay out our hospital program."

The AFC national committee took no official stand on term extension, largely because its chairman, General Wood, did not want to be put in the position of challenging the army chief of staff. Many local chapters, however, strongly resisted the proposals.

While taking no official stand on the conscription controversy, the

AFC promoted the slogan "National Defense at Any Expense, But Keep Our Boys at Home." It denied the possibility of invasion from Europe; therefore it saw no justification for U.S. entry into combat zones along the coasts of Northern Ireland, Scotland, or Norway. Furthermore, it denied that such potential "trouble spots" as Iceland, Siberia, Dakar, the Azores, and Cape Verde were really in danger. After examining all the supposed routes by which the United States could be invaded, the AFC found the nation well protected. (*See Document No. 20.*)

As in the original debate over the draft in the summer of 1940, the anti-interventionists offered a major alternative: a return to the volunteer system. General Wood called for a special reenlistment bounty, suggesting $150 per man. If a sufficient number could not be induced to reenlist, special provision could be made to keep draftees in such places as Hawaii, Panama, and Trinidad from three to six more months.

A Close Call. The bill's sponsors encountered difficulties. On August 7, by the comfortable margin of 45 to 30, the Senate offered only an eighteen-month extension, provided for a pay raise after one year's service, and sought to expedite the release of men over age twenty-eight. On August 12, the House narrowly passed the same bill, 203–202. Furthermore, the vote has often been misunderstood. Even if the eighteen-month extension had been turned down, undoubtedly a compromise would have been reached, and draftees would still have had to serve from six to twelve more months. On the very day of the House vote, the president was involved in a secret rendezvous where, for the first time, he would come face-to-face with his British counterpart.

CHAPTER 7

TOWARD CONFRONTATION

Atlantic Conference. From August 9 to 12, Roosevelt and Churchill, together with their military staffs, met covertly at Argentia Bay off the Newfoundland coast. Their discussions focused on defeating Germany and staving off Japan, though in the long run even greater value lay in the personal ties established between the two leaders. To the American public, the main product of the meeting was the Atlantic Charter, a joint declaration of Anglo-American war aims. Somewhat reminiscent of Woodrow Wilson's Fourteen Points, the charter abjured any territorial desires and expressed the determination to destroy Nazism. It called for freedom of the seas, self-determination for all peoples, equal access to the world's trade and raw materials, improved living standards, the disarmament of aggressor nations, and ultimately "the establishment of a wider and permanent system of general security."

Anti-interventionist Reaction. Many anti-interventionists were suspicious on two counts. First, they suspected that the Newfoundland meeting involved secret U.S. commitments to enter the war directly. Second, they thought the statement of peace aims was either dangerous or unworkable. Flynn surmised that the Charter was a "cover-up" for secret interventionist schemes. Congressman George Holden Tinkham (Rep.-Mass.) considered charging Roosevelt with treason; the president had made "a declaration of war, without Congress, on a British battleship." Journalist Chesly Manly of the *Chicago Tribune* accused the two leaders of plotting a military invasion of the European continent. Boake Carter saw the encounter smacking of "the sort of secret Hitler-Mussolini meetings at the Brenner Pass, where the two dictators blandly decided how many lives should be carved up to accomplish their aggressive purposes." Norman Thomas envisioned the United States ending up fighting to protect British Singapore or the Dutch East Indies. AFC staffer Ruth Sarles thought American troops might be sent to Liberia or Sierra Leone.

As far as the Atlantic Charter went, a few FDR critics praised the document. Such pacifists as Oswald Garrison Villard, Frederick J. Libby, and Dorothy Detzer saw genuine grounds for hope. General Wood thought the Germans might be receptive. Congressman Louis Ludlow saw the ground cut from under Hitler.

A few other anti-interventionists found it so weak that it was meaningless. To Senator Nye, it was "a lot of words." Retired diplomat William R. Castle called it a "rehash of old ideas." Claiming that the belligerents would ignore the manifesto once the war ended, Hearst said, "You can galvanize a dead duck but you cannot bring it to life." The *Christian Century* stressed the specific verbs used in the Charter's Eight Points: hope, encourage, desire, wish, will endeavor, will aid. The framers, in other words, had really committed themselves to nothing.

Point by point, the anti-interventionists offered a critique. Hearst listed an entire group of nations for whom the eight points would not apply, among them India, Persia, Egypt, and Arabia. The AFC research bureau had doubts concerning the points dealing with territorial change or the restoration of popular sovereignty. (*See Document No. 21.*) The *New York Daily News* asked if equal access to resources obligated the U.S. to remove all immigration and tariff barriers. The *Chicago Tribune* denied that Roosevelt had authority to commit his nation to "the final destruction of Nazi tyranny." Railroad lawyer John Finerty, soon to be national KAOWC chairman, claimed that it not only called for disarming Germany; it also sought to break up that nation, something that would only reinforce Hitlerism, not destroy it. *America*, the Jesuit weekly, found the Charter's terms requiring Anglo-American policing of the entire world. To *Uncensored*, the document was as hollow as a political platform. (*See Document No. 22.*)

The *Greer* Incident. On May 21, 1941, over two months before Roosevelt and Churchill met in the Atlantic, the Germans sunk their first U.S. ship. The *Robin Moor*, a merchant vessel flying the American flag, was headed for British South Africa. It carried material defined as contraband by the Germans, the British, and the United States itself. No lives were lost.

Then, on August 17, the *Sessa* was shelled near Greenland. It was transporting foodstuffs, lumber, and other general cargo to Iceland, presumably to supply the U.S. Marines who had landed there in July. Twenty-four members of its crew were lost, including one American.

Because, however, of its Panamanian registry (a standard U.S. subterfuge), the *Sessa* technically was not a U.S. ship at all and hence not entitled to the protection of the American flag.

On September 5, the U.S. freighter *Steel Seafarer*, flying the American flag, had been bombed in the Red Sea while en route to an Egyptian port. There were no fatalities. In reacting to all three sinkings, the AFC stressed the contraband issue and accused the administration of allowing U.S. seamen to find themselves at risk.

Roosevelt, however, bided his time until September 11. Then he told a nationwide radio audience that, exactly one week earlier, the American destroyer *Greer* had been fired upon by a German submarine while carrying American mail to Iceland. Mentioning as well the attacks upon the *Robin Moor*, *Sessa*, and *Steel Seafarer*, FDR found "a Nazi design to abolish freedom of the seas, and to acquire absolute control and domination of these seas for themselves." The next German steps: "domination of the United States, domination of the Western Hemisphere by force of arms" as part of their ultimate goal—"world conquest and permanent world domination by sword." To ward off "the rattlesnakes of the Atlantic," American ships and planes would henceforth "strike their deadly blow—first," that is they would shoot on sight and ask questions afterwards. Furthermore, American patrolling vessels and planes would "protect all merchant ships—not only American ships but ships of any flag—engaged in commerce in our defensive waters." Roosevelt did not say so, but the previous inclusion of Iceland within the Western Hemisphere zone meant that "American defensive waters" were now extended to some 400 miles off the Scottish coast. For roughly three-quarters of the Atlantic, therefore, American vessels would escort friendly convoys, in the process eliminating any Axis forces encountered on the way. An undeclared war in the Atlantic had officially begun. Following FDR's speech a Gallup poll indicated 62 percent support.

The Anti-interventionists Response. Minutes before the president's address, Lindbergh addressed an AFC rally at Des Moines. In his broadcast, carried by radio throughout the nation, he condemned Hitler's persecution of the Jews but labeled Jews, along with the British and the Roosevelt administration, as among the three major elements leading the nation to war. "Their greatest danger," he continued, "lies in their large ownership and influence in our motion pictures, our press, our radio, and our Government." Immediately, he—and the AFC—

were called pro-Nazi, anti-British, and above all anti-Semitic. Within a month he and the AFC denied such accusations, but his address dealt the AFC a blow from which it never recovered.

Still in all, the anti-interventionists were quick to respond to the president's speech. *Uncensored* stressed that the *Greer* was sunk in the German war zone while steaming to U.S. troops stationed at the British war base of Iceland. The United States had been needling Germany, said the *Chicago Tribune*, by sharing the occupation of Iceland with the British. To the *Christian Century*, the incident did not match in magnitude the Japanese attack on the *Panay*, an incident that took place on the Yangtse River in December 1937 and that was peacefully resolved.

On October 14, the chief of naval operations, Admiral Harold Stark, released an official report, in which he noted that the *Greer* had sought out the German sub, trailed it doggedly for hours, and given British planes information to facilitate their attack. Nye said, "What the German submarine did was probably less than we would have done under like circumstances." Congressman Usher Burdick asked, "Just what does the President think the commander of the German submarine should have done, when chased for several hours by a destroyer?" Hoover called the *Greer* "the aggressor." The *New York Daily News* denied that Roosevelt possessed "an overwhelming respect for truth as truth."

As far as FDR's shoot-on-sight orders were concerned, the anti-interventionists were even more furious. General Wood reproached the president for initiating "an undeclared war, in plain violation of the Constitution." A detailed AFC position paper accused FDR of violating the 1939 Neutrality Act, misrepresenting "freedom of the seas," and eliminating Congress as a policymaking body. (*See Document No. 23.*) Anne Morrow Lindbergh concurred: "An amazing speech," she wrote in her diary. "A wizard he is to make so plausible the thesis that we will continue to give all possible aid to the enemies of Hitler while being affronted if Hitler does not respect our rights as a 'neutral'!"

Other Sinkings. The sinkings did not cease. On September 11, 1941, the very day FDR gave his shoot-on-sight speech, the *Montana*, en route to Iceland, was torpedoed 260 miles southwest of that nation. Chartered to a private American firm, it was registered under the Panamanian flag. No American was on board. On September 19, the *Pink Star* was sunk between Greenland and Iceland under almost identical circumstances. The AFC again responded, branding Nazi submarine warfare "unquestionably ruthless" but attacking the whole subterfuge of Panamanian registry. (*See Document No. 24.*)

Although Roosevelt was already implementing his convoy orders, on September 27 still another sinking took place. A German U-boat had struck the *I. C. White*, a tanker that belonged to the Standard Oil Company of New York but was flying the Panamanian flag. Sailing alone from Curacao to Cape Town with a cargo of fuel oil, it was hit some 600 miles east of Pernambuco, Brazil. Three of its crew were lost, all Americans.

FDR Seeks Neutrality Revision. On October 9, Roosevelt went even further. His "shoot-on-sight" orders had concerned military vessels; now he was addressing himself to commercial ones. He urged Congress to repeal the "crippling provisions" of the 1939 Neutrality Act. Specifically, he proposed the arming of American merchant ships, a move that he claimed would make it possible for the United States to defend the Hemisphere far more successfully. Furthermore, aid would be delivered with greatly increased effectiveness against the "tremendous forces now marching toward conquest of the world." The president did concede that "the arming of merchant vessels does not guarantee their safety," but he continued that "it most certainly" added to it. Though not on his immediate agenda, he expressed the general wish that Congress would give its "earnest and early attention" to eliminating the ban on entering combat zones, thereby permitting American merchant ships to reach belligerent ports. FDR denied that he was calling for a declaration of war; he was, he said, simply concerned with the "essential defense of American rights."

Critique of FDR's Armed Ship Proposal. Anti-interventionists were quick to respond. General Wood accused FDR of urging that American ships be sent into "submarine-infested war zones." The president, the AFC leader claimed, was "asking Congress to issue an engraved drowning license to American seamen." Congressman Robsion recalled that within thirty days after the United States had armed its ships in 1917, it entered World War I. Moreover, anti-interventionists saw such arming as not protecting American seamen but endangering them. Representative Paul Shafer (Rep.-Mich.) made the analogy of sending "a 10-year-old boy out into the jungles to hunt ferocious tigers

with a slingshot." Congressman Short compared the proposal to a box-
ing match between comedian Eddie Cantor and heavyweight champion
Joe Louis.

The AFC's criticism of FDR's proposal was detailed and extensive.
According to its researchers, there was great difficulty in firing guns on
the restless deck of a moving ship, particularly when aircraft or U-boats
were in the vicinity. Furthermore, armed merchantmen made easy tar-
gets, for in convoys the fastest ship must travel at the speed of the slow-
est. Congressman Frank Crowther (Rep.-NY.) noted that the United
States only possessed 400 four- and five-inch guns, most nearly forty
years old and many of which had proven unsuccessful in World War I.
Then there were the prevailing shortages, which made it impossible to
arm 200 ships in a merchant marine of some 1,200 vessels. Those craft
would invariably face German subs, even on the American side of the
Atlantic. The AFC quoted British officers as denying efficacy of such
protection, as it was too difficult to coordinate the whole crew of a ship.
The experience of World War I was recalled. Armed ships then could
not defend themselves, even though U-boats and aircraft were far less
efficient. And if all these factors were not enough, the AFC claimed that
such arming violated international law. Once a merchant ship was
armed, it lost all immunity as a neutral vessel.

Continued Debate—and Sinkings. As the Senate began debate, two more merchant ships were sunk. On October 16, both the
W. C. Teagle, a large Standard Oil tanker, and the *Bold Venture* went
down. The two ships were en route to Britain, carried Panamanian registry, and were hit some 500 miles south of Iceland. No American lives
were lost on either. On the next day, October 17, the Navy Department
announced that the U.S.S. *Kearny*, a crack destroyer, had been torpedoed. Coming to the aid of some fifty merchant ships that had left a
Canadian port in convoy early that month, it was struck by German
subs about 400 miles from Iceland. The ship was damaged, not sunk.
But eleven lives were lost, the first American fatalities on an American
ship before Pearl Harbor.

Such incidents, particularly the attack on the *Kearny*, all had their
effect. On October 17, the House, voting 259 to 138, permitted the
arming of U.S. merchant ships. Two days later, a Gallup poll showed 72
percent favoring the arming of merchant ships, 53 pecent for entering
combat zones. Now the matter lay before the Senate.

Responding to the House action, on October 18 Hitler publicly confirmed secret orders: "If . . . an American ship shoots . . . it will do so at its own peril. The German ship will defend itself, and our torpedoes will find their mark."

In the meantime the sinking of merchant ships continued. On October 19, the freighter *Lehigh*, bound from Bilbao, Spain, to the African Gold Coast, was sunk without warning some 75 miles off Freetown—an area not staked out as a combat zone by any belligerent. All thirty-nine crew members were rescued by a British destroyer. The ship belonged to the United States lines, flew the American flag, and was carrying only ballast.

This time anti-interventionists found Germany totally in the wrong. Villard called the sinking the "one absolutely indefensible case." To Vandenberg it was "the act of a wanton pirate," to Wheeler "a foul crime." Taft warned that if the practice continued, "we shall have a cause for war."

On October 27, in a Navy Day address, Roosevelt claimed that with the attack on the *Kearny*, an American war vessel, the nation itself had been attacked. Furthermore, so he told his radio audience, he possessed a secret map that revealed Hitler's plans to weld South and Central America into five vassal nations. Moreover, he had covert evidence that Hitler planned to abolish all existing religions and establish an international Nazi church.

Anti-interventionists were quick to respond. Much of the argument centered on the *Kearny*. Hoover noted it was "convoying British ships—not even American-flag vessels." Said Senator Wheeler, "The *Kearny* gave chase; she tossed off depth charges; she was out for the kill." To Borchard, "The indignation at her being torpedoed is nauseating." Congressman John M. Vorys (Rep.-Ohio) found the sinking was all the more reason to defeat the armed ship bill. If a submarine could sink a well-armed destroyer such as the *Kearny*, just what chance had tramp steamers, armed with guns of World War I vintage?

Roosevelt's opponents questioned his claims concerning Nazi designs. General Wood noted the president's refusal to public inspection of the presumed Nazi documents. The *Chicago Tribune* asserted that sweeping contingency plans, such as FDR said the Germans possessed, were hardly surprising. Indeed every general staff in the world had studied every conceivable type of military action against every conceivable enemy. Were Roosevelt to examine American War and Navy Department files, he could find plans for attacking Britain and seizing Canada.

The Senate bill was especially crucial, for not only did it permit the arming of merchant ships, it gave them permission to enter war zones. Former senator David A. Reed (Rep.-Pa.) found it the most critical decision Congress faced since 1861. The *New York World-Telegram*, a Scripps-Howard paper, called it "a vote on undeclared naval and air war." The *Christian Century* entitled its editorial "The Last Stand."

As the Senate debated its version of Roosevelt's proposals, two more ships were sunk. On the night of October 29–30, the armed U.S. navy tanker *Salinas* was torpedoed southwest of Iceland while traveling in convoy. There was no serious injury, much less loss of life, and the *Salinas* reached port safely. On October 31, a far more pivotal incident took place, for a German U-boat torpedoed the U.S. destroyer *Reuben James*, part of a five-destroyer escort, six hundred miles west of Ireland. Of the 160 men on board, only 45 were rescued. Roosevelt condemned the sinking, but took no further action.

Roosevelt's critics gave familiar arguments. Congressman Robert Rich (Rep.-Pa.) accused the government of "committing murder on the men in our own Navy contrary to our own form of government." Amos Pinchot, long known as a reformer in the Progressive mold, said, "We can't expect the Germans to refrain from doing what we would do in their place." Nye remarked, "The sinking had about as much to do with the defense of our shores as the sinking of a freighter by an iceberg."

On November 7, after eleven days of bitter debate, the Senate voted 50 to 37 to arm U.S. merchantmen and permit the entry of U.S. ships into war zones. The legislation then went back to the House, which had to rule on the war zone issue.

Not surprisingly some House members spoke in apocalyptic terms. Knute Hill (Dem.-Wash.) said the vote really involved a declaration of war. George A. Dondero remarked, "This will be the last vote before we enter the second World War." William Pfeiffer (Rep.-N.Y.) envisioned American ships entering such far-flung areas as Murmansk, the Black Sea, and the Suez Canal.

To the anti–interventionists, such efforts were unnecessary. Wheeler claimed that Germany was a far less dangerous power in October 1941 than it had been a calendar year earlier. Taft found the British possessing many more ships than the United States, relative tonnage being 25 million tons to only 4 or 5 million. In fact, according to the America

First Committee, England had more shipping than when the war began.

In the minority report of the House Foreign Affairs Committee, one alternative was presented: placing all such American merchant ships under British registry. Such a move, said the anti-interventionists, would do several things at once. It would eliminate the embarrassment of registering U.S. ships under the Panamanian flag, provide Britain with American merchant ships, leave the option of their being armed to the British, and above all save American lives.

Admiral Stark challenged the opposition. Manpower in Britain, he said, was at a premium. Moreover, American crews would operate American ships more efficiently, keep them in better condition, and get more speed out of them, for they obviously had the greater familiarity. Furthermore, the United States must reserve the authority to send its own ships at will, particularly as it needed essential resources from all areas of the world.

Roosevelt was taking no chances. He sent a special communication to the House Democratic leadership, saying that U.S. convoys in combat zones would save both time and money. And he got his way, for on November 13, the House voted 212 to 194 to eliminate the war zones. For practical purposes, the Neutrality Act of 1939 was dead.

In this vote, the AFC had mobilized its maximum strength. A shift of ten legislators would have defeated the measure. General Wood noted that those members of Congress opposing revision represented about half the nation's voters. Moreover, the margin was far too narrow to encourage FDR in asking for an outright declaration of war, even if the president was so inclined.

On the same day the bill was passed, Hitler held a naval conference in which he approved a new set of orders for German "surface forces." If American naval vessels began action, including the "shadowing" of submarines, the German commander must not be "too late in using his weapons."

Some anti-interventionists still hoped that outright war could be avoided. To the *Christian Century*, the very closeness of the vote might slow Roosevelt down. Flynn thought the president would wait at least a month before using his new powers. The AFC's liaison to the House found the narrowness of Roosevelt's margin "a genuine and effective moral victory."

Others, though, were less optimistic. The *Chicago Tribune* entitled its editorial "The Vote for War." Hiram Johnson remarked, "We'll be fighting the whole war soon." *America* magazine noted that "Minus a formal declaration, we are launched squarely and solidly into the war."

Even in late November and early December, however, Roosevelt remained cautious. On November 22, with characteristic ambivalence, he spoke of creating routes to Britain and Russia. "The use of American flag ships must come very soon," he said, "but should be worked into gradually." Three days later, it was decided that American vessels traveling to Lisbon should not be armed, but that U.S. merchant ships bound for Archangel needed such protection. In giving his orders Roosevelt asserted, "Ships under the American flag go to Great Britain as soon as they become available but that this procedure progress gradually with only a small number of ships being so routed in the beginning. This number may be increased at a later date if in accordance with Administration policies and instructions." Presumably, these vessels would have been included in British convoys, thereby postponing a decision about whether to send a convoy of U.S. ships under U.S. escorts. The orders were not publicized—hardly the all-out effort to provoke war that Churchill believed that FDR promised him in August. If the president was trying to protect the Atlantic supply line, he was doing so in the least provocative way.

Of course, in the end, it was Hitler who would decide what constituted provocation. But the German Führer was never in any hurry to start a war with the United States while his European problems remained unsettled. The Japanese attack on Pearl Harbor would soon make the issue a moot one. All during the crisis, however, the anti-interventionists were devising ways to protect the nation militarily and economically.

CHAPTER 8

TO PROTECT A NATION

Continental Defense. Many anti-interventionists, like their pro-administration counterparts, deplored the nation's military weakness, indeed hammered incessantly on the issue. Yet they claimed that a properly organized defense, one centering solely on the Western Hemisphere, could make the United States invincible. When interventionists warned that the United States could well go the way of Poland, Finland, and France, their critics challenged them point by point. Often cited was the report of the Senate Committee on Naval Affairs, released in June 1940. Chaired by the anti-interventionist David I. Walsh, the committee reported that the United States could be defended by guarding vital air and sea approaches. Furthermore, argued many anti-interventionists, Hitler's continual conquests only weakened him. Because he would be forced to spread his occupation forces thinly indeed, it would be difficult enough for him to keep control of the European continent.

To anti-interventionists, a continental defense was not only possible; it was the most desirable of all strategies. Proper allocation of U.S. resources would enable all of North America and much of South America to be protected. Moreover, within the hemisphere lay practically every raw material needed to fight a modern war, including rubber (which could be developed in Brazil) and tin (which lay in Bolivia).

Anti-interventionists continually referred to the Monroe Doctrine, a century-old manifesto that proclaimed "hands off" to any European military activity in the Western Hemisphere. Certainly most saw North and Central America, not to mention the Caribbean, as in the U.S. sphere of influence. At times a bit of demagoguery was manifested, as when Senator Lundeen called for simply grabbing the European-owned islands of the West Indies, supposedly in lieu of debts still owed from World War I. Martinique, Bermuda, the Bahamas, Guadeloupe could all be U.S. territory. "Quit stalling—just take them," said the *New York Daily News* in speaking of France's possessions, but for a few anti-interventionists the sentiment had much wider application.

Equally obviously, however, the demand struck a ready chord among anti-interventionists—and some others as well. There was more at work than mere vengeance upon an "ungrateful" Europe. There was a legitimate fear, one shared in fact by the Roosevelt administration, that Hitler's conquest of European nations would cause him to claim their possessions in the New World, many of which lay in the Caribbean.

Bases were deemed particularly crucial. In June 1940 Charles A. Lindbergh called for placing military enclaves "wherever they are needed for our safety, regardless who owns the territory involved." He endorsed U.S. bases in Colombia, Venezuela, the Guineas, the Galapagos islands, and the Amazon valley. The *Chicago Tribune* was not adverse to a base at Pernambuco, Brazil. Even the Socialist Norman Thomas spoke in terms of Cape Verde and the Canary islands.

One anti-interventionist blueprint was found in *Strategy of the Americas* (1941) by Fleming MacLiesh and Cushman Reynolds, who often wrote for the liberal weekly *Common Sense*. The two authors cited the maxim of Frederick the Great: "If you defend everything, you defend nothing." Rather than seek to protect the entire hemispheric land mass, the United States should establish a huge ring of hemispheric bases ranging from Greenland and Newfoundland to Para and Pernambuco in Brazil. Hanson Baldwin's *United We Stand!* presented similar recommendations, calling for military outposts from Labrador to the shoulder of Brazil.

To many anti-interventionists, military control of at least parts of Latin America was crucial. General Wood believed that the United States must insist "that no government in Mexico, Central America and the Caribbean countries will be tolerated unless it is friendly to the United States and that, if necessary, we are prepared to use force to attain that object."

Other anti-interventionists stressed limits to the U.S. presence. Castle maintained that the United States might have to use force to quell "disturbances" in the Caribbean and Central America. Complete protection of such nations as Brazil and Argentina, however, he found far beyond U.S. capacity. Hearst called the South American nations a military liability. Hugh Johnson saw problems in defending a continent composed of suspicious and hostile nations.

Air Power. Most anti-interventionists were adamant in seeking domination of the air. Indeed Senator Lundeen, Major Williams, and the *New York Daily News* were not alone in asking that the War and Navy Departments be matched by a new, autonomous, and powerful Department of the Air Force. In one sense the argument was simple:

although no foreign power was able to conduct continuous bombardment of the United States, the United States in contrast could easily
pick off any attacking aircraft. It is the nation that controls the air, said
Senator Wiley, which "carries the big stick." To the *Chicago Tribune*, the
long-range bomber was America's number one defensive weapon. To
MacLiesh and Reynolds, the United States needed "an air power great
enough to make the skies untenable for any person who dared to come
against us." Al Williams wrote that the nation that ruled by air would
"rule the world." The title of his book on the subject: *Airpower* (1941).

Yet even for many holders of such views, air power was no panacea.
In examining the role air power had in the first two years of the European war, they found it effective only when supported by infantry and
tanks. In discussing Hitler's blitzkrieg against Poland and Western
Europe, the *New York Daily News* remarked, "Bombing did not topple
those countries; the infantry did." During the recent civil war in Spain,
General Wood claimed, the bombardment of cities alone did not win
the conflict. The *Chicago Tribune*, in turning to the Finnish war, noted
that the Russians had dropped 6,667 bombs only to kill a grand total of
eighteen civilians.

Navy. Anti-interventionists were more divided on the role of the
navy than on air power. Senator Walsh saw salvation lying in the battleship alone. The *New York Daily News* continually called for a "two-
ocean navy," that is massive American fleets on both the Atlantic and
Pacific. Those of like mind denied that the United States could be out-
produced in any naval race, even if the Germans captured the British
fleet.

There was, however, no unanimity in the rank of FDR's critics. Fish,
for example, strongly opposed major naval increases, finding such forces
obsolete. Colonel McCormick found a "one-ocean" navy quite sufficient, for if navies from both major waters struck the United States, it
could defend on one side and attack on the other.

A Mobile Army. Almost all anti-interventionists doubted the
wisdom of a large army. A new American Expeditionary Force would
simply prolong the struggle overseas, work against needed negotiation
between England and Germany, and ultimately ensure Soviet domination of Europe. In their eyes, the war of maneuver, used so recently and
so successfully by Germany, had made huge numbers of ground forces

obsolete. While the German blitzkrieg obviously influenced such think-ing, undoubtedly memories of millions slaughtered in the trenches of northern France were also a factor. Hence they pushed for small, highly trained forces. Even the *New York Daily News*, which favored the initial 1940 conscription bill, stressed the need for "master mechanics," trained in trucks, tanks, and electrical equipment. True, anti-interven-tionists often used the fall of France to call for a crash defense program, but for them genuine defense involved the strengthening of hemisphere deterrents, not foolish diffusion of U.S. forces overseas.

In brief, to the foes of intervention, bases throughout the Western Hemisphere, a superior air force, a navy fit for the high seas, and a de-fensive, technically trained army could ably protect the nation.

German Economic Competition: An Administration Anxiety. As long as the debate over intervention lasted, the Roosevelt administration continually stressed that Germany was not only a mili-tary threat. It was an economic one as well. In his speech declaring a national emergency, given on May 27, 1941, the president warned that the Nazis sought the economic strangulation of North America. Ameri-can workers and farmers, no longer able to export what they produced, would see living standards lowered. Not only would wages and hours be "fixed by Hitler"; "the whole fabric of working life as we know it—business, manufacturing, mining, agriculture—all would be mangled and crippled." Just over a week before, Cordell Hull had warned of an entire world economy manipulated by the Nazi commercial weapon of barter. "The would-be conqueror," said the secretary of state, "forces delivery to him, at his own price, of the goods he wants; and enforces this arrangement by every device of discrimination and arbitrary con-trol."

Other interventionists offered similar concerns. In August 1940 Dorothy Thompson, columnist for the *New York Herald Tribune*, main-tained that German victories would create "the largest free trade area and the largest planned economy in the world." Given the dominance of the German mark and the supremacy of German barter techniques in such regions as Latin America, the United States itself would be bound to become an economic colony of the Reich. Douglas Miller, for-mer U.S. commercial attaché in Berlin, wrote an entire book entitled *You Can't Do Business with Hitler* (1941). Here he warned that German economic strangulation would force an isolated United States to adopt the one thing feared by all of American business: state socialism. Besides, Miller asserted, loss of the critical materials—found in abundance in the Old World—might create dangerous deficiencies in the American defense program.

Anti-interventionist Answers.

Several anti-interventionists also had economic anxieties. Governor Alfred Landon of Kansas, Republican presidential candidate in 1936, saw a lower American standard of living inevitable. In January 1941, Joseph P. Kennedy, who had just resigned as United States ambassador to Britain, claimed that another year of war would cause the U.S. to lose all foreign markets.

Yet, to all such anti-interventionists, the economic cost of intervention was too high. Merle Thorpe, editor of *Nation's Business*, asked, "When has war helped a nation's trade in the long run?" War, said Senator Taft, destroys more in one year than the United States could benefit in twenty. Furthermore, it was asserted that the United States could effectively retaliate against German dumping and barter techniques. "This is a game at which two can play," said Senator Henry Cabot Lodge. Even the fact that competitors paid much lower wages did not necessarily harm American sales. The factories of China, India, and the Malay states all used cheap labor, Wheeler acknowledged, but the United States was still able to contend successfully.

Indeed, according to a few foes of intervention, a British victory would be just as damaging commercially to the United States as a German one. A triumph by either power, claimed *Uncensored*, would restrict U.S. trade, for their war-ravaged economies would need to use government-controlled barter techniques in order to survive. Congressman James O'Connor (Dem.-Mont.) claimed that even a triumphant Britain would be so "bled white" that it would have to give its own dominions tariff preferences. Pacifist leader A. J. Muste foresaw an intensive British-U.S. war for markets in the offing.

Some anti-interventionists maintained that a German victory might actually benefit the United States. Indeed, Germany's very expansion would give the United States economic leverage it would not otherwise have. To Senator Nye, a German victory might even improve American prospects as Britain, "our chief competitor," would finally be removed. By cooperating with "a Europe dominated by Germany," commented Charles A. Lindbergh in August 1940, "we can maintain the supremacy of our western civilization and the right of our commerce to proceed unmolested throughout the world." In his book *Hell-Bent for War* (1941), Hugh Johnson claimed that the nation's unmatched industrial plant, raw materials, and gold supply gave it, not the Axis powers, the commanding position. Similarly General Wood saw the relatively self-sufficient United States having the natural advantage. Indeed, John T. Flynn found Hitler's Greater Germany absolutely dependent upon the outside world.

John Chamberlain, one of the few anti-interventionists on the staff of Henry R. Luce's *Fortune* magazine, claimed that the United States was the only great power that unquestionably could survive alone. In his book *The American Stakes* (1940), Chamberlain said that the United States was still in a seller's market, being the only country that could specify its own commercial conditions without having to fight for them. If the current war ended in high tariffs, autarchy, and bilateral barter throughout the world, the United States could lend Europe sufficient gold to enable that continent to reorganize on lines of free commerce. He wrote, "We do not need to fight and demobilize our own economy in order to put our weight behind sound moves toward a Manchesterian world."

The AFC Research Bureau drew upon a report from an apparently unimpeachable source, the highly respected Brookings Institute, to advance its most provocative claim: namely that a Nazi-dominated Europe would be extremely vulnerable to American pressure. (*See Document No. 25.*) Similarly, George N. Peek, former manufacturer of farm implements and New Deal agricultural administrator, asserted the United States could bargain to advantage. (*See Document No. 26.*)

Anti-interventionists also had a fall back position: autarky. According to Hoover, the United States was 93 percent self-sufficient and in a pinch could be 100 percent so. By applying labor-saving devices, fostering capitalism as a system, and maintaining free competition, the nation could not only meet competition but continue to sell abroad. Joseph P. Kennedy saw the United States 95 percent self-sufficient already, Nye 97 percent. If worse came to worse, said Kennedy, "we could gear ourselves to an intelligent self-contained national economy and still enjoy a fair amount of prosperity." To economist Stuart Chase, the United States was the most integrated continental empire in the world, producing half the world's industrial output and having ready access to all the raw materials it needed.

In a book entitled *America and a New World Order* (1940), General

Motors executive Graeme Howard called for the economic division of the world into six blocs—continental Europe, the British Empire, the Soviet Union, Latin America, North America, and Japan's "New Order for Asia." True, Howard conceded, the United States would find keen competition from Britain, Germany, Italy, and Japan, all of whom needed foreign markets in order to survive. It could, however, sell such agricultural goods as cotton, lard, tobacco, and wheat, while supplying loans for productive projects.

Latin America's Economy Debated. Often anti-interventionists debated the role Latin America would play in their vision of economic integration. Some emphasized the difficulties involved, particularly in dealing with the southern half of the South American continent. They readily acknowledged, for example, that such exports as cattle—produced in abundance by Argentina, Uruguay, Brazil, and Chile—competed with U.S. agricultural products while finding massive markets in Europe. Of all Latin America's major exports, both agricultural and mineral, the United States took only coffee in bulk. Conversely, European-made manufactured goods were bought widely. D. Worth Clark remarked, "One might as well dam up the cataract as to stop the normal channels of international trade." Hoover made a similar point, declaring that "the world has to live," even if "our South American cousins" needed to sell agrarian surpluses to totalitarian blocs. If South America could not trade with the Axis powers, said John T. Flynn, it was "sunk."

Hence many anti-interventionists opposed any hint of the heavy hand. The United States, insisted Chicago business leader Sterling Morton, should never force goods "down the throats of our South American neighbors." Free-market economist Frank Chodorov asked if the U.S. fleet would chase German merchantmen from South American waters if the United States was undersold. Irrespective of who won the war, commented Norman Thomas, no nation had the right to cut off the vast supplies of South America from the rest of mankind. To compete with Europe for South American trade, warned the *New York Daily News*, the United States must subsidize its exports or cut its own workers' wages "to the bone." The United States could no more get rich swapping its cattle, oil, and wheat for Latin America's than "the proverbial laundresses could get rich taking in one another's washing."

Yet few anti-interventionists wrote off the continent altogether. Several claimed that strong ties already existed. Major Al Williams found the entire hemisphere "the true zone of American commercial and military influence." The United States, the AFC noted, already possessed "the lion's share" of trade with that region, doing as much business there as Germany, England, France, Italy, and Japan combined. "Why shouldn't we continue to do so?" it asked. America First chairman General Wood concurred. "We stand today in an unrivaled position," he said. "The reorganization and proper development of Mexico alone would afford an outlet for our capital and energies for some time to come."

In his book *Pan America: A Program for the Western Hemisphere* (1940), journalist and Latin American expert Carleton Beals offered an entire schema for economic integration. Effective hemispheric policy needed, he said, far more than denunciation of international aggression and defense of an exploitative status quo. He suggested a host of policies: inter-American control of the Panama Canal, local ownership of raw materials, guaranteed preferential markets for the United States, reprisals against nations that "favor European nations at our expense," preparation for political independence or statehood for Puerto Rico, plebicites for the people of the Virgin Islands, and cancellation of British and French debts whenever these nations set their New World populations free. In addition, he wanted return of the Falkland Islands to Argentina and of British Honduras to Guatemala and Mexico. There should, Beals went on, be no change in the economic or political status quo of the Americas without joint Pan-American agreement. While continually calling for hemispheric self-sufficiency, he warned that Latin American nations could no longer be seen as "our oyster to be devoured, or as shock troops for our safety, or as pawns in the game of world politics."

To several anti-interventionists, German barter techniques were no threat. Those Latin American nations who traded with Hitler's Reich, so Hugh Johnson predicted, would soon possess an overabundance of aspirin, bicycles, and cameras. "Ignorant nations will no longer trade tusks of ivory and wedges of gold for calico, squarefaced gin and strings of beads." In countering Douglas Miller's argument concerning the lack of raw materials, many anti-interventionists stressed the self-sufficiency of the Western Hemisphere. "We need not," the AFC research bureau said, "go to war for rubber or tin; American boys need not fight and die in Dong Dang or Bangkok."

In anti-interventionist eyes, proper preparation could deter any military and economic threat from abroad. Still at issue, however, was the war itself and how to end it.

CHAPTER 9

ALTERNATIVES TO WAR

Eradicate Nazism by War: An Impossibility. Several anti-interventionists denied that military conquest of Germany could eliminate the ideology of Nazism. Congresswoman Jessie Sumner (Rep.-Ill.) asked, "Can you reform people by shooting and gassing them?" Oswald Garrison Villard asserted that real cleaning of Germany must come from within: "Only the Germans can do away with the Nazis and their totalitarian state." "Behind Hitler," warned Hugh Johnson, "are substitute quarterbacks."

To Anne Morrow Lindbergh, a vast revolution was at work, one that could not be stopped by any "hopeless" crusade to "save" civilization. (*See Document No. 27.*) When critics accused her of condoning fascism as the inevitable "Wave of the Future," she responded vigorously. In the June 1941 issue of the *Atlantic Monthly*, she wrote unequivocally:

I look with horror on those evils we see in Europe; the suppression of free speech, free action, the relinquishing of individual rights to the control of one man, the end of democratic government, the wielding of hate as a weapon, the unrestricted use of force and terror, mob riots, class warfare, racial and religious persecution.

The Wave of the Future, she maintained, was no inevitable wave of communism, fascism or Nazism to which Americans must "bow down in abject subjection." Rather it was "a movement of adjustment to a highly scientific, mechanized, and material era of civilization, with all its complications." Though the Europeans had been overwhelmed by this Wave, the United States could guide it, that is "taking advantage of that wave and controlling it with all the powers at your disposal." She found the early reforms of the New Deal such an "attempt to meet and ride this Wave of the Future, and, as such, was greeted with hope by a majority of forward-looking people." Were the United States to launch itself blindly into the war, all possibility of imposing order on the chaos of a revolutionary era would vanish.

Germany's Weakness. To many anti-interventionists, however, the more territory Germany conquered, the weaker it became. Hugh Johnson quoted Napoleon's maxim: "Empires always die of indiges-

73

tion." Wheeler found the European continent too diverse ever to be molded into a single unit. Even if Germany conquered all of Europe, so Hanson Baldwin argued, it would still confront major problems. It would face the mistrust of Russia and Italy, find the domination of conquered peoples uneasy, and experience the exhaustion resulting from any war. To Alfred Landon, the problem of permanently occupying such "free, courageous, and patriotic people" as the French, Dutch, and Norwegians was insurmountable. Colonel McCormick drew from the entire span of human history, ranging from the Athenians at Syracuse in 413 B.C. to the Russians in Manchuria in 1905, to prove that nations undertaking distant military adventures always experienced great catastrophe.

Even if Germany did remain victorious, the United States could survive. Speaking in August 1940, Charles A. Lindbergh said, "In the future we may have to deal with a Europe dominated by Germany. . . . An agreement between us could maintain civilization and peace throughout the world as far into the future as we can see." Besides, there were precedents for living with dictators. In the past, said the *New York Daily News*, the United States had lived alongside Czarist Russia ("a black tyranny") and Abdul ("the Damned") Hamid II, the late nineteenth-century Ottoman ruler who had massacred his own people.

The Folly of Invading Europe. During 1941 most anti-interventionists found any invasion of the European continent almost insuperable. Comparisons were made to World War I. In January 1941, Wheeler recalled that a quarter century earlier Germany had been able to stave off an army of at least two million Frenchmen and a million English plus vast forces on the Russian flank. When the United States was fighting earlier, noted Fish in April, it had twenty allies on its side plus the protection of the British, French, Japanese, and Italian fleets.

Logistics alone appeared insurmountable. In May the *Chicago Tribune* found transportation problems overwhelming. Even if an American Expeditionary Force was organized in Britain, winning a foothold on the continent would be "the most bloody and expensive business in the history of war." The occupied peoples, fearing the inevitable devastation to come, would meet invaders' forces only with apathy and hostility.

By the end of June 1941, Germany was fighting on two fronts, but even the entry of the Soviet Union into the conflict did not change anti-interventionist analyses. Late that July the New York AFC chapter claimed that five to six million Russian troops could not beat the Germans on their own soil. How possibly could American forces fighting three to four thousand miles away from their own bases? In August the *New York Daily News* predicted the United States would have to supply 420 divisions to make an invasion feasible. It warned, "It is possible that our boys may suffer one or more super-Dunkirks rather than enjoy a victory march to Berlin. And the Atlantic Ocean is a trifle wider and harder to evacuate large forces across than is the English Channel." In November Frank Gannett, who owned a chain of newspapers in New York State, asked, "How can we get across the Atlantic with no place to land our troops, and defeat the Nazis?" That same month editor Frank Waldrop saw no safety from air attack. "Where could we spread out and form our armies for maneuver?" he asked.

Even during the second half of 1941, with heavy fighting on the Russian front, projected invasion figures were indeed awesome. In October John T. Flynn saw four to five million troops needed. Freda Utley saw six to seven. In November Bennett Champ Clark spoke of eight, Henrik Shipstead of six to eight. In early December *Catholic World* editor James Gillis used the figure ten million.

Negotiated Peace Favored. To anti-interventionists continuation of the war was sheer suicide, leading only to unequaled devastation. Hence, they believed, the United States must foster some sort of negotiated peace. Throughout the entire conflict, calls were continually made for negotiation, mediation, or at least an armistice. During the time of the phony war, a variety of mediators was suggested, including Pope Pius XII, the monarchs of Belgium and the Netherlands, and Benito Mussolini.

Before suspicions of Roosevelt really took hold, mediation by the president was endorsed by many anti-interventionists. Among them were some who would soon be opposing him bitterly, including Hugh Johnson, Senator Nye, *Uncensored*, and the *New York Daily News*. Those anti-interventionists who were particularly influenced by pacifism wanted FDR to initiate a settlement, including the Keep America Out of War Congress, Norman Thomas, and Oswald Garrison Villard.

Even after the destroyer-bases deal, FDR's name was mentioned. In November 1940 General Wood suggested Roosevelt or the pope. As late as May 1941, Wheeler told a New York AFC rally that the president "could bring about the peace of the world."

At first Roosevelt himself expressed some curiosity about possible peace bids. In February 1940 he met with William Rhodes Davis, an independent oil entrepreneur, who told the president about his visit in October with Hermann Goering. The Nazi leader had told Davis that Germany would welcome FDR's presence at a general peace conference that would liquidate the Versailles settlement and redistribute colonies. Roosevelt was momentarily interested but found little of merit in the supposed bid.

Also early in 1940 Roosevelt asked James D. Mooney, vice president of General Motors, to use his high German contacts to see if Berlin sought "a fair and equitable solution." Roosevelt claimed if the belligerents genuinely sought to reconcile their differences, he was ready to act as mediator. Nothing came from the journey though henceforth Mooney continually called for a negotiated settlement.

In February and March 1940 Undersecretary of State Sumner Welles visited Europe at Roosevelt's behest. Although the mission was simply to report on current conditions, several anti-interventionists— including such disparate voices as the *Christian Century* and William Randolph Hearst—were most enthusiastic.

Others were skeptical. The *Chicago Tribune* was reminded of Colonel Edward M. House, President Wilson's emissary in 1916, who sought to commit the United States to the Allied cause. Herbert Hoover smelled a vote-getting ploy timed for the 1940 elections. Congressman Paul Shafer personally attacked Welles, who was admittedly the stereotype of the urbane polished diplomat. He hoped that the dapper emissary would not "put on those English clothes which are pressed and kept by his British valet, and ask that we sing God Save the King instead of My Country 'Tis of Thee."

Welles saw little ground for optimism. Both Germany and the Allies, he soon learned, sought victory, the British and French foreseeing no lasting peace until Nazism itself was abolished. Besides Welles may well have exceeded his orders by attempting to act as mediator. According to historian Irwin F. Gellman (*Secret Affairs* [1995]), FDR genuinely sought information only.

When, on May 10, 1941, Deputy Führer Rudolph Hess made his mysterious flight to Britain, more peace talk commenced. Headlined *Peace Action*, the voice of Frederick J. Libby's NCPW, "Peace Discussions, Not Peace Negotiations, Have Begun." Wheeler asked FDR to call a peace conference. The *Chicago Tribune* spoke of Hitler's desire for peace, based on his fear of military stalemate and his desire to fight the Soviets. Hess, however, was strictly on his own and certainly did not speak for Hitler.

Several anti-interventionists suggested concrete terms. In mid-December Wood suggested independence for Norway, Denmark, Belgium, and the Netherlands, and the retention of the British empire. Late that month 1940 Wheeler spoke of the restoration of Germany's 1914 boundaries; the return of Germany's former colonies; an autonomous Poland and Czechoslovakia; the re-establishment of an independent France, Netherlands, Norway, Belgium, and Denmark; the return of Alsace-Lorraine; protection of all religious and racial minorities; internationalization of the Suez Canal; and arms limitation. Such a peace would not include indemnities or reparations.

In March 1941, the *Christian Century* offered even more Wilsonian aims. (*See Document No. 28.*) One of the more publicized efforts came from Congressman John Vorys, who in the spring of 1941 called upon the United States to launch "a peace offensive." (*See Document No. 29.*)

That May investor Sterling Morton mentioned the restoration of Norway; the "semi-independence of France"; the transfer of Alsace-Lorraine to Germany; German domination of the Balkans; a German interest in the Suez Canal; and German hegemony over Italy and its colonies. In October advertising executive Chester Bowles listed complete political independence for France, Belgium, Denmark, and Norway; German withdrawal behind its former frontiers, which could possibly include Alsace-Lorraine; and the reestablishment of the British and Italian Empires to their prewar status. The political and economic future of Central and Eastern Europe, including national boundaries, would be fixed by a conference of the powers involved. Neither Hitler, Mussolini, nor Churchill would participate in the negotiations.

Much of the time, anti-interventionists conceded that the realities of the battlefield made a restoration of Europe's 1939 boundaries impossible. Britain, they hoped, would preserve its empire intact, but they acknowledged that Germany would remain dominant over Europe. To Charles A. Lindbergh, speaking in early winter 1941, no peace that had a chance of actually being negotiated could include the restoration of the Polish Corridor or "the former status quo" in Czechoslovakia. The aviator denied that he would "particularly approve" of a German-dominated peace or "call it just, by our standards," but he saw the only alternative "a disastrous war." Similarly General Wood found German economic control of Western Europe inevitable. Alfred Bingham, coeditor of liberal monthly *Common Sense*, did not find a continent dominated by Hitler "a pleasant prospect to look forward to, but it is at least possible that we shall have to make the best of it as the most we can hope for."

Several rationales were offered for such peace sentiment. One centered on the sheer havoc created by continued strife. If the conflict continued, warned Senator Edwin C. Johnson, "millions of women and children will be starved by the blockades, millions of men slaughtered at the front, and billions of taxpayer's money will be squandered. While such a fire rages no one's peace will be safe." During the same month Senator Bulow called upon France and Britain to accept Hitler's bid of October 6, 1939, in which the German dictator said he would make peace if the Allies accepted his domination of Poland. "A poor treaty is better than a good war," said the South Dakota Democrat. "It may not be to our liking, but let them do the best they can and save some millions from destruction." Another anxiety concerned the bolshevization of Europe. If war continued, claimed the *New York Daily News* in January 1941, Europe would become "a likely hunting ground for Bolshevism." A wider rationale was given by journalist Freda Utley. (*See Document No. 30.*)

If Roosevelt ever toyed with the idea of mediation during the phony war, as historian Robert Dallek (*Franklin D. Roosevelt and American Foreign Policy, 1932–1945* [1979]) suspects, he totally abandoned all such notions once Western Europe fell. In his fireside chat of December 29, 1940, he asked: "Is it a negotiated peace if a gang of outlaws surrounds your community and on threat of extermination makes you pay tribute to save your skins?" A negotiated peace, he maintained, would be "no peace at all," but "only another armistice, leading to the most gigantic armament race and the most devastating trade wars in all history."

Other interventionists felt similarly. In April 1941 columnist Dorothy Thompson stressed that Hitler had never adhered to any pact, sought complete domination of Europe, and would not even permit a free Britain to exist. Seven months later Senator Joseph Ball (Rep.-Minn.) found any negotiations leaving the Nazis in control of Europe, thereby only serving as a breathing spell in the ongoing conflict. In January 1941 a Gallup poll revealed close to 80 percent favored British pursuit of the war until Germany was defeated. Only 15 percent endorsed a truce.

So long, though, as the war continued, anti-interventionists not only called for settlement. They maintained that outright American participation would destroy the very domestic foundations of the nation they knew.

CHAPTER 10

A MATTER OF SURVIVAL

Enter the Hoagland Family. In November 1939, the illustrated weekly *Look* offered a four-page picture essay on the Hoaglands, "an average middle-class family in a city of 100,000 inhabitants." According to the scenario, the United States enters the war on the side of the Allies. Almost immediately a totalitarian state begins to emerge. At the small textile plant where he works, Mr. Hoagland is visited by an army officer who directs him to make military uniforms. Government boards start dictating output, purchases, selling price, and even labor relations. Strikes are forbidden. So is the switching of jobs. Both food and electric power are rationed, so the Hoaglands eat often by candlelight. With inflation raising prices faster than wages, the Hoaglands soon find themselves unable to pay rent and are evicted from their home. Twenty-year-old Jim Hoagland is drafted, then shot in combat; one of Jim's brothers and a sister take war jobs while still another brother, yet in high school, is forced to wear a uniform. To escape arrest for owning such banned pacifist literature as Hemingway's *Farewell to Arms*, the family burns its own books. Movies, radio programs, the very mail it receives, are censored. Children with German names are stoned by boys on the block while "rebels" experience strict surveillance by a new secret police. After the armistice, the nation sinks into depression. The younger members of the Hoagland household family lose their jobs as Mr. Hoagland's business suffers from low prices and no demand. The general point of the saga: "Dictatorship in America is no longer a remote nightmare."

The *Look* article was based upon a volume edited by Larry Nixon, news editor for the New York radio station WNEW, and entitled *What Will Happen and What to Do When War Comes* (1939). In the anthology, C. Norman Stabler, financial editor of the *New York Herald Tribune*, described how war would affect industry. As in World War I, Stabler commented, gasoline, coal, sugar, and wheat would be rationed. Electric power would again be rationed, so as to save coal, thereby forcing office workers to walk up entire flights of stairs and sit at their desks with overcoats on. In the coming conflict, plants producing such "nonessentials" as lipstick would be forced to produce such "essentials" as medical supplies. Other economic consequences would include reckless government buying; increased insurance, interest, and tax rates; limitation of essential imports; and inflation of the currency.

Civil liberties too would vanish. W. W. Chaplin, daily news commentator for Hearst's International News Service, offered an list of what would disappear: "Free speech, free press, free assembly, the profit system, labor organizations, the party system of government, perhaps Congress and the Constitution itself." In Nixon's book, Chaplin described a police state in the offing:

After you have been reprimanded a few times for loitering, for lighting a cigaret during a blackout, for violating any one of a hundred petty restrictions, you will begin to walk with an eye cast over your shoulder, you will talk even about the weather in a whisper, you will suspect even your best friends of being spies or agents of the secret police.

M-Day. The story of the Hoaglands, together with the analyses of Stabler and Chaplin, illustrate one attitude that both conservative and liberal anti-interventionists shared: participation in war would place America's very survival as a free republic in jeopardy. Of particularly great concern were the various war mobilization plans drafted in Washington. Anti-interventionists often referred to M-Day or Mobilization Day, the moment when the United States would go on a complete wartime footing and all of American life would be regimented. Such contingency preparations had been proposed by Washington officials in 1931, 1933, and 1936, though none had the sanction of law. The purpose of such thinking was obvious: to avoid the mistakes of World War I by having a full-scale mobilization blueprint on hand if the need arose.

In early August 1939, Roosevelt established the War Resources Board (WRB), chaired by United States Steel board chairman Edward Stettinius, Jr. It was commissioned to deal with almost all the problems characteristic of a modern wartime economy: production, labor, prices, materials, transportation, and agriculture.

The formation of the WRB frightened anti-interventionists of all political persuasions. Church editor Harold E. Fey wrote, "Dictatorship is being definitely planned for the United States." *Uncensored* foresaw the lowering of wages and the banning of political meetings. Congressman Roy Woodruff (Rep.-Mich.) found the scheme mobilizing "every man, woman, and child" in America; it was "designed necessarily" to set aside the Constitution and the Bill of Rights. Bennett Champ Clark, the board's most prominent congressional critic, warned that business leaders would be told either to adhere to government-set priorities or see their enterprises ruined. According to Flynn, M-Day codes, inevitable in wartime, would remain after the fighting stopped, particularly as the United States would see its economy reduced to the very kind of disorder that characterized Italy in 1922 and Germany in 1933.

The board's report, completed on October 12, was relatively innocuous. It called for a number of temporary wartime agencies that could be promptly disbanded when the emergency was over. In fact, little was done about its recommendations. But, to foes of FDR's foreign policy, all such proposals remained haunting indeed.

National Regimentation. Even if the United States faced no M-Day, war always brought one thing in its wake: centralized executive power. Conservatives saw the capitalist economic system itself in peril, as full-scale mobilization was bound to bring in its wake inflation, price and wage controls, compulsory unionism, and—in practicality—a wartime socialism that would remain after the conflict ended. Nationalization could well be in store, with all industry, capital, and labor under the thumb of the new Socialist state.

For those who already deplored the rash of New Deal government controls, the future was indeed ominous. Taft saw private enterprise and local self-government in ruin. Private property, feared Borchard, might become "a thing of the past." Morton, envisioning the disappearance of private industry, spoke in terms of a "staggering blow" to civilization, a "new Dark Age." In an obvious bid for labor support, the AFC research bureau warned that the eight-hour day might be eliminated. And with an eye to the housewife, it claimed that to save power and maximize production, even washing machines might be banned. Herbert Hoover, who had been a major federal administrator in World War I, claimed that during that conflict the United States became an effective dictatorship. "Every month," he wrote, "we tightened the clamps of fascism—we did not know the word then—tighter and tighter."

Those of a more reformist bent, however, were equally concerned. To anti-interventionists of the left, war would eliminate all hope of a radical, and in their eyes more rational, reorganization of the economic system. For years after World War I, wrote Norman Thomas and his fellow Socialist Bertram D. Wolfe (*Keep America Out of War: A Pro-*

gram [1939]), "big business remained in the saddle where the logic of war put it."

One voice of alarm followed another. To pacifist Milton Mayer, U.S. entry into the war would "destroy democracy as we have it as a nation." To John Haynes Holmes, entering the conflict meant "burning down the house to get rid of the rats." War, the Unitarian minister continued, could destroy American liberties far more than could Hitler. Senator La Follette predicted that American workers would be given a stark choice: either work where the government directed and under government-controlled conditions or experience starvation. Harry Elmer Barnes did not find "Communist totalitarianism" out of the question.

Fear of War Boom. Several anti-interventionists used the language of guilt in speaking of any newfound prosperity. In September 1939 the Roman Catholic lay periodical *Commonweal* referred to "the dance of the ghouls during the first session of the stock market." An editorial in the *Christian Century* began: "Wall Street and the wheat pit are off on a joy-ride." A month and a half later, Flynn referred to the "thrill of hope" expressed by financial gamblers upon hearing of British maritime disasters.

Others claimed that any war boom was bound to be artificial. In March 1941, *Uncensored* suspected that armament production could not absorb all workers displaced from such industries as autos. Middlemen too would suffer, while in the meantime consumers could only be able to buy second-hand cars, refrigerators, and radios. That September the AFC noted factory shutdowns—a zipper firm in Meadville, Pennsylvania; a refrigerator plant in Evansville, Indiana—as the government diverted materials from nonessential industries. In November Wheeler predicted the complete paralysis of the construction industry and marked unemployment in such enterprises as autos, silk, cork, and rubber.

Ultimately economic depression was inevitable. Here again left and right shared deep fears. Nye spoke in terms of "ghostlike" communities, whose new industrial plants would suddenly become empty. Farmers too would suffer, for overseas markets would decrease while their crops drew less income at home. Advertising executive Chester Bowles foresaw "millions of disillusioned soldiers and sailors looking for an early delivery on the rainbow they were promised." Economist

Maynard Krueger, Socialist candidate for vice-president in 1940, and Senator Lundeen thought conditions would be so bad that dictatorship would result. Charles A. Lindbergh was even more apprehensive: "God knows what will happen here before we finish it [World War II]—race riots, revolution, destruction."

Several anti-interventionists stressed the national debt. General Wood feared an obligation of $150 billion by the end of the war. Eddie Rickenbacker, World War I flying ace and president of Eastern Airlines, spoke of $200 billion. The *New York Daily News* simply said, "We'll all be busted."

Domestic Poverty. All this time, several anti-interventionists argued, domestic ills were being neglected. To them, the real war was the war against poverty. As Norman Thomas commented, "We have more refugees from our own dust bowl than there are refugees from Finland." Senator La Follette referred to 10 million unemployed, while Representative Burdick saw 62 million Americans impoverished.

The interventionists, some asserted, had their priorities awry. Senator Capper claimed that the cost of one "Stop Hitler" advertisement would provide two weeks at a summer camp for scores of slum children. Noting food shipments to British youth, Congressman Robsion asked how many American children were without milk and chicken. Robert M. Hutchins, president of the University of Chicago, listed a host of domestic problems that he saw needing immediate attention, ranging from alleviating unemployment to insuring civil liberties. (*See Document No. 31.*)

Civil Liberties. To some anti-interventionists, particularly the liberals among them, the possible loss of civil liberties was most frightening. According to Harry Elmer Barnes, long-held rights would simply become a "dolorous memory." In wartime, said Senator Wheeler, "every foreign accent becomes the sound of the devil." Even the far more conservative Hamilton Fish predicted that war would terminate civil liberties within forty-eight hours. In November 1941 Socialist leader Maynard Krueger made a telling reference to the rise of Nazi Germany; the United States, he claimed, was already in its "Brüning" stage, referring to a German chancellor who preceded Hitler.

To those so concerned, signs of intimidation appeared everywhere. The wording of proposed anti-subversive, anti-sabotage, and anti-alien legislation appeared far too loose. In 1940 Norman Thomas pointed to the recently passed Smith Act, which made it unlawful to advocate or teach the overthrow or destruction of any government in the United States by force and violence. In noting the provision making "promotion of disaffection" in the armed forces a crime, the Socialist leader thought that any criticism of the government's foreign policy could be prohibited. In 1941 *Uncensored* warned of censorship administered through a newly established Office of Government Reports.

The Federal Bureau of Investigation (FBI) was severely criticized. *Uncensored* accused its director, J. Edgar Hoover, of being "a grown man with a cops-and-robbers mind," who had spied on "U.S. Senators, Cabinet members, and diplomats." Flynn claimed Hoover ran his own Gestapo. Nye accused the FBI of helping to create a war scare centering on foreign agents.

Conversely the America First Committee sought FBI help in purging its organization of subversives. Lindbergh, upon being told that the FBI was tapping his phone, said he would be glad to speak "more plainly" and clarify any remarks the agency could not understand.

Certain instances gave little comfort. Some anti-interventionist letters to FDR were turned over to the Criminal Division of the Department of Justice, the FBI, and the Secret Service. Efforts were made, at times with success, to prevent AFC meetings from being held. For example, in May 1941, the Carnegie Institute of Technology denied Philip La Follette, former governor of Wisconsin, the right to address an AFC meeting there. Similar events occurred regarding the Philadelphia Music Hall, Brooklyn's Ebbets Fields, and municipal auditoriums in Atlanta and Oklahoma City. In October 1941, when Norman Thomas was scheduled to speak at the University of California–Los Angeles, the provost there banned his appearance. Even the Fraternal Order of Eagles, usually seen as a benign group, denied Wheeler a hall while he was on a speaking tour in California.

In short, to the anti-interventionists, war would produce such social strain that the United States would have difficulty surviving. A nation remaining at peace, however, could yet organize its resources so as to preserve its republican form of government and advance its prosperity. Ironically, such decisions concerning the fate of the nation would be made neither in Washington nor in Berlin but in far-off Tokyo.

CHAPTER 11

THE PACIFIC CHALLENGE

Confrontation Opposed. Beginning in July 1937, Japan engaged in an undeclared war with China. By the end of 1939 Japan held many of China's major cities—including Peking, Shanghai, and Nanking—and much of the interior as well. Americans, seeing newsreels of bombed populations and starving refugees, were outraged. In 1939 a Gallup poll taken revealed 66 percent willing to boycott Japanese goods, 72 percent favoring an arms embargo on Japan.

Many anti-interventionists were among those strongly opposing Japan's actions. As early as 1938, Japan's activity in China had reminded Herbert Hoover of Genghis Khan. James Gillis spoke of "prodigious slaughter." Norman Thomas called the China conflict "both a crime and a blunder."

Pacifists in general and many "isolationists" wanted all trade in war materials severed. Indeed such important members of Congress as Nye had long spoken on the subject. Yet among the anti-interventionists who were the most visible and vocal, many others opposed exercising any commercial pressure on Japan. As the AFC said in November 1940, "We sympathize with China. But we must not plunge America into war . . . for sentimental reasons."

Several anti-interventionists put the issue in terms of immediate national interest. Japan's activities, they said, did not threaten the United States. Its policy in China, said the *Chicago Tribune* in September 1939, was solely "an Asiatic question," one having no effect on the Western Hemisphere. In August 1941, the New York chapter of the AFC conceded that the Japanese were "behaving badly to China," but it asked: "But what has she done to us? How has she offended us? How has she attacked us?"

A few anti-interventionists even praised the Japanese role in Asia. According to jurist John Bassett Moore, China had gone "from bad to worse," whereas "Japan has, by her own efforts, steadily risen." Sterling Morton claimed that Japan had restored peace and order to large sections of the former Chinese empire.

Other anti-interventionists found Japan itself in some ways victimized, for impersonal economic pressures made life difficult for the island nation. The *Christian Century* noted that Japan's 70 million people, crowded 473 to the square mile, would not starve quietly. Asked pacifist Kirby Page, "In Japan's shoes would American patriots be less aggressive and belligerent than the Japanese are now?" Senator Wiley stressed Japan's need for raw materials, markets, and a greater income.

War Scenarios. Several anti-interventionists denied that Japan offered any military threat to the Western Hemisphere. In October 1939, Senator Holt commented caustically, "I suppose she [Japan] is going to fly her big tanks over the Canadian Rockies. Or if she cannot fly them over, she will outfit all the Japanese soldiers with snowshoes so they can climb over the mountains in the winter time and get at us in that way."

During 1940 several anti-interventionists—ranging from the pacifist Frederick J. Libby to the more militaristic William Randolph Hearst—saw Japan too preoccupied in China even to think of war against the United States. Harold E. Fey, returning in December 1940 from a trip to the Far East, reported that Japan was experiencing such economic depression it could not even sustain the China campaign.

To anti-interventionists, Japanese invasion was a sheer absurdity. Senator Downey denied that Japan could launch a blitzkrieg on the West Coast, for any such effort required five to ten times the strength used against China. Even if Japan used every ship in the nation, it would be unable to convoy, much less supply, the 100,000 troops needed. According to Taft, 200,000 U.S. troops stationed on the Pacific coast could prevent any Japanese landing. Conversely, Japan ran the risk that the U.S. fleet might slip back into the Pacific and destroy its entire forces.

In particular, anti-interventionists denied the existence of any Japanese naval threat. In October 1939, Bennett Champ Clark pointed to a three to one preponderance in naval power. Fish estimated the U.S. Navy as 30 or 40 percent larger than Japan's. Holt quoted the comment of Admiral Harry Yarnell, commander-in-chief of the Pacific fleet: "The inhabitants of the Pacific coast can sleep quietly in their beds until Japan builds a navy twice the strength of the United States."

By the same token, American conquest of Japan would be most difficult. *Uncensored* envisioned a costly blockade that might last for years.

Senator Walsh warned that a battle in the eastern Pacific might prove "naval suicide": the greater the distance from its support base in Hawaii, the more hazardous the engagement. In the scenario of Major Al Williams, Japan would not fight the American fleet "in Nelson style"; rather it would wait until after its air and submarine forces had trimmed down American sea power.

A land invasion of Japan was portrayed as well-nigh impossible. Operating out of its own bases, possessing submarines, airplanes, and armies, the island empire could destroy any expeditionary force long before it arrived on its shores. Even if American troops started out from Hawaii, it would take from three to four bloody years to occupy Pacific islands some eight hundred miles away from Japan. In *United We Stand!*, Hanson Baldwin claimed the feat would take a million men. True, according to the *New York Times* staffer, the United States would probably win, but the conflict would be "a long, hard, grueling war of attrition," leaving "a trail of blood across the Pacific." Frederick J. Libby spoke in terms of $50 billion and a five-year struggle. Even then, said the pacifist leader, the United States might still be fighting on the Chinese mainland, finding itself actually defeated or seeing communism sweep all over east Asia. To the *New York Daily News*, victory itself was futile: "Unless we sterilize them, they will proceed to breed, half-starve, hate, and build up new armaments, and in due time the 'yellow peril' will bounce up again, more perilous than ever before." In advocating United States-Japan conciliation, William R. Castle feared an exhausting struggle on both sides. Castle felt he was speaking with some authority, for he had been U.S. ambassador to Japan from 1929 to 1941. (*See Document No. 32.*)

Given the existing tensions with Germany, several anti-interventionists warned against fighting a costly two-front conflict. A few suspected that Roosevelt would create a crisis with Japan in order to manipulate surreptitious U.S. entry into the war. Such a maneuver, they stressed, was to no one's advantage except perhaps the Axis. Even if Germany did not come to Japan's aid, the United States could get sidetracked in a Pacific debacle while British cities were still being pounded.

China, according to some anti-interventionists, was no paragon of virtue. The word dictatorship was frequently used to describe the rule of Generalissimo Chiang Kai-shek. Wheeler found no more democracy in China than in British India or Malaysia; Taft saw no more than in Brazil or Greece. Hearst stressed communist influence within the country. Editor Burton Rascoe called China's ruler "a cheap gangster." Because the Generalissimo had married into the wealthy Soong family, Rascoe claimed Chiang "would sell out, as he has sold out, time and again, for the perpetuations of the futures of his wife's family."

The lively U.S. trade with Japan was frequently brought up. Hugh Johnson noted, "We seem to be ready to sacrifice $400,000,000 of our annual Japanese trade to protect $100,000,000 of big business fixed investment in China." To Hanson Baldwin, the United States would be "cutting its nose to spite its face" to fight Japan in order to preserve the rest of its trade in the Orient. Investment counselor William J. Baxter wrote an entire book on the topic *Japan and America Must Work Together* (1940).

At the same time, possible profits from a free China were much denigrated. In February 1941 lumber merchant George Cless stressed that Americans had invested less than $50 million in China, "slightly more than we paid for chewing gum last year." Boake Carter found the total American financial stake in China amounting to less than what was spent annually on athletic events. "It seems grotesque to fight the good customer on behalf of the not so good customer," remarked the *New York Daily News*.

The Philippines. The Philippine Islands were a U.S. possession slated for independence in 1946. Until then, however, it held the status of commonwealth under U.S. sovereignty. In 1934, Congress had passed the Tydings-McDuffie Act, which targeted Philippine independence in twelve years, provided for the removal of American military posts, and envisioned negotiation with the Filipinos over naval bases.

Although the War Department had long held that the islands were a military liability, several anti-interventionists stressed their importance. Hearst, for example, warned that any American departure would only result in Japanese occupation. Wheeler claimed he would favor war if they were invaded.

Such voices, however, were a decided minority. In their effort to avoid conflict with Japan, most anti-interventionists were quite willing to find the Philippines expendable. Norman Thomas called the Philippines America's Achilles heel. Both *Uncensored* and the AFC saw them as a "headache" to American strategists. Hanson Baldwin stressed that the islands lay behind a screen of Japanese mandates. According to the *New York Daily News*, the islands would serve as "the graveyard of a lot of valuable American man-o'-warsmen and men-o'-war." The American navy, said Hugh Johnson, would be engaged some six thousand miles from the American continent, its striking power thereby trimmed by two-thirds. Even if such a discrepancy were offset by a vast preponderance of tonnage, chances of victory were most uncertain.

Furthermore, so anti-interventionists argued, the Filipinos themselves sought a quick severing of ties. For years, said the *New York Daily News*, its inhabitants had been "begging us to let go." The *Chicago Tribune* pointed to the American tradition of bestowing freedom upon subject peoples. Harry Elmer Barnes noted that many members of the Philippine assembly were pro-Japanese, that economically the Japanese were extremely powerful there, and that the so-called Spanish "tycoons" who controlled the important industries were pro-fascist.

According to the anti-interventionists, there was little American economic stake there. Hugh Johnson asserted that the American taxpayer paid three dollars for every one received in benefits. Frank Waldrop said, "They aren't worth enough to justify a war."

Guam. In February 1939 Congress had voted down a five million dollar appropriation to construct harbor works on Guam, a U.S. possession. Administered by the Navy Department as an outlying naval station, Guam was some 3,850 miles from the natural Alaska-Hawaii-Panama defense line. Both the State and War Departments disparaged the harbor proposal, feared that the move would antagonize Japan. Hearst, Hanson Baldwin, and the *New York Daily News* favored its fortification, but most anti-interventionists were opposed.

Cost was a factor. So was location. Retired General William C. Rivers, who often spoke against intervention in Asia, argued that the cost of such a base would exceed more than the total U.S. stake in the entire Far East, including its many investments. The *Chicago Tribune* saw the United States "sticking its neck out." Moreover, it was argued, fortification was provocative. Such a move, said Libby, was comparable to reciprocal action by Japan in the Galapagos Islands or by Germany in Bermuda. "Stop this madness," he wrote in his monthly bulletin *Peace Action*.

Southeast Asia. To the anti-interventionist, Southeast Asia represented one thing: Western domination. In January Norman Thomas accused FDR of "policing the Far East for the benefit of American imperialism over Japanese imperialism." By July 1940, the *Christian Century* feared that the United States was becoming the receiver in bankruptcy for the colonial possessions of Britain, France and the Netherlands. That October the *New York Daily News* attacked the presence of the British in Hong Kong, Malaya, and India, saying that they had "no more historic or racial right to be in any of these places than the Germans have to be in France." The New York AFC chapter accused Britain of being "parked" in Asia for its gold, oil, rubber, silver, diamonds—rich materials that its capitalists had stolen from the Asian people. William Henry Chamberlin asked, "How many Americans, on a referendum vote, would choose to die for the Dutch East Indies, for Singapore, for Thailand or Senegal?" He sardonically continued, "I am anticipating the day when the possession of Tibet and Afghanistan will be represented as vitally necessary to the security of Kansas and Nebraska."

Interventionists often claimed that the United States was dependent upon Southeast Asia for strategic materials. Could the nation exist, it asked, without the rubber of Malaya, the oil of the Dutch East Indies, and the tin of Indochina? Administration critics continually sought to meet this argument. More than sufficient oil, they claimed, lay in North and South America. As far as rubber was concerned, U.S. chemical companies had been producing a durable, pliable substitute at one-third the cost. Furthermore, rubber plantations were starting up in South America. The tin of East Asia could be replaced by that produced in Bolivia. Otherwise, feared Congressman Cliff Clevenger (Rep.-Ohio), "little white crosses, row on row," might well "stud the tropic miasmic swamps of Sumatra and Java, in the interests of the tin can and rubber tire." Better to replace "the tin-plated can with one of silver in an emergency and come off financially better than to engage in a military adventure based on Singapore."

Besides, so the anti-interventionists argued, a Japan dominant over Southeast Asia would still need the American market. Over 50 percent of the world's rubber and tin, said Hugh Johnson, was consumed by the United States. The Japanese would be unlikely to toss away half the business of that region. In the words of the *New York Daily News*, "If we play ball with Japan, Japan will play ball with us, commercially at least. It always has."

Anti-interventionist Alternatives. During the entire crisis several anti-interventionists offered alternatives to administration pressure. Those with pacifist leanings were particularly articulate. Norman Thomas favored mediation. The *Christian Century* called for a world conference. The FOR wanted a customs union for Pacific and American people. The NCPW envisioned progressive American resumption of trade in return for military restraint. The WIL called for the withdrawal of all foreign troops and extraterritorial rights in Asia, repeal of the Oriental Exclusion Act of 1924, and adequate trade agreements.

Other anti-interventionists too made suggestions. Historian Arthur J. May proposed neutralizing the Philippines. Sterling Morton wanted to exchange U.S. recognition of Japan's position in Asia for Japan's recognition of the Monroe Doctrine in the Western Hemisphere. Columnist George Sokolsky suggested a Pan-Pacific conference. China, Japan, Britain, the Soviet Union, and the Dutch East Indies would all attend and FDR would preside.

Economic Pressure Opposed. On January 26, 1940, the United States abrogated a commercial treaty with Japan made in 1911. Henceforth trade would be on a day-to-day basis, always at Washington's mercy. If the United States believed that Japan was endangering its interests, it could issue retaliatory restrictions.

Until war broke out, anti-interventionists feared that the administration would start levying embargoes. To Senator Wiley even an arms embargo would "be taking sides"; the action would prompt Japan to blockade Chinese ports, shut out all imports, apply martial law wherever its armies were located, and exclude all foreigners from China. Herbert Hoover found that shutting off scrap iron and octane gas exports was simply "sticking a pin in a rattlesnake," as Japan would simply purchase these items elsewhere while becoming embittered against the United States. Indeed the severing of oil alone, claimed Libby, would merely cause Japan to conquer such areas as Borneo.

William Henry Chamberlin, who had written *Japan Over Asia* in 1936, found that the advocates of sanctions lacked any knowledge of elementary psychology. In the May 1941 issue of *Harper's Magazine*, Chamberlin said, "A regime that bowed to economic pressure, openly exercised, would stand little chance of being able to continue to govern its own people." The aggressive regime would simply take sanctions in its stride or "strike out with at least a sporting chance of victory."

Iron and Steel Embargo. On September 26, 1940, Roosevelt banned the exporting of scrap iron and steel outside the Hemisphere (except for Great Britain), a move clearly aimed at Japan. The event took place only five days after Vichy France had given Japan permission to maintain three air bases in Tonkin, Indochina, and to maintain a small force at Haiphong.

Anti-interventionists saw no reason for FDR's move. "What have we to do with Indo-China, with which we have comparatively little trade, which is under a Government in France for which we have no overwhelming sympathy?" asked Castle. The *Chicago Tribune* suspected that Roosevelt made the move in order to create a war that would assure his victory in the 1940 election. Morally, the newspaper insisted, there was no difference between France's original "grabbing" of the territory and Japan's current move.

Tripartite Pact. On September 27, 1940, Japan entered into an alliance with Germany and Japan. In a treaty signed in Berlin, Japan recognized German and Italian leadership in the creation of a "new order in Europe." In return Germany recognized a Japanese new order in "greater East Asia." The three powers pledged mutual assistance, by military and other means, if one of the three was attacked by any power not involved in the European or Sino–Japanese war. There was one qualification: existing relations with the Soviet Union were not to be affected.

Most anti-interventionists believed the United States had reaped the consequences of its own folly. Nye blamed the administration for "driving Japan into the arms of those who were the last ones we wanted her associated with." Wheeler warned the United States to stop its attacks "on every other nation." "We must," he continued, "be careful not to get into a two-ocean war with our one-ocean navy." The *Christian Century* claimed that the Axis was simply responding to the possible American occupation of naval bases in Singapore, the Dutch East Indies, South Africa, and Sierra Leone. Oswald Garrison Villard pointed out other Japanese anxieties, such as those centering on a possible base on Guam, the assumption of England's interests in the Pacific, appropriations to build a two-ocean navy, and American protests concerning the status quo in Indochina and the Dutch East Indies. Professor Borchard conceded that the pact was the first military alliance ever formed against the United States. At the same time, the Yale professor found it "a perfectly natural response to the underlying error of conducting foreign policy on a basis of denunciation, chastisement, embargo, boycott, threat and an alleged moral superiority."

Freezing Japan's Assets. For the rest of 1940 and well into 1941, Japan sought to tighten its grip on Indochina and gain a foothold in the Netherlands East Indies. On April 13, 1941, just a little over two months before Hitler invaded Russia, Japan concluded a neutrality pact with the Soviet Union. On July 23, the Vichy government of unoccupied France permitted Japan to build eight air and two naval bases in southern Indochina.

On July 26, acting together in response, the United States and Britain froze all Japanese assets. Two historians, William L. Langer and S. Everett Gleason (*The Undeclared War, 1940–1941* [1953]), found this move "probably the crucial step in the entire course of Japanese-American relations before Pearl Harbor." A day later, Roosevelt placed the armed forces of the Philippines under U.S. command. Japan responded by freezing U.S. and British assets. On August 1 a complete U.S. oil embargo on Japan existed.

Anti-interventionists became jittery indeed. Senator Wheeler approved of the freezing order but warned against battling Japan to preserve British domination of Asia. The *Chicago Tribune* asked, "Are we to fight Japan for good old Singapore and Queen Wilhelmina?" Castle noted that the United States certainly would not refuse to trade with Britain if, as was frequent, it had offered its "protection" to some small nation or colony. Borchard mused, "I wonder what difference it will make to an Indo-Chinese whether a French General or a Japanese General occupies the thatched hut in Cambodia." To the New York City AFC, the administration was proposing a "new and dangerous doctrine," for it was construing an attack on the United States itself whenever one foreign power acquired bases of another foreign power.

Final Negotiations. On November 5, the Japanese government announced that veteran diplomat Saburo Kurusu was en route to Washington on a special peace mission. As the U.S. embargo, particularly in the area of oil, was increasingly effective, tensions were becoming acute. In advancing arguments offered by many anti-interventionists, the *New York Daily News* saw no issue that could not be resolved. (*See*

Document No. 33.) The *Christian Century* found the proposals advanced by the American negotiators far too one-sided. (*See Document No. 34.*)

All peace talks, however, proved futile. On November 26, Hull submitted his final proposals. They included the withdrawal of Japanese armed forces from China and Indochina, the mutual withdrawal of trade restrictions, the unfreezing of Japanese assets, and a nonaggression pact among the Pacific powers—Japan, the United States, China, the Netherlands, the Soviet Union, and Thailand. The United States had long cracked the Japanese diplomatic code and hence knew that the Japanese negotiators were simply stalling. Hull himself conceded that his terms were strictly "for the record" and that war was only a matter of time.

Early December marked the final few days of peace. Everywhere there was tension. The *New York Daily News* found the United States slipping into war without the public being informed as to the negotiations. Congressman William P. Lambertson (Rep.-Kan.) warned, "It would be foolish for us to go into Japan to defeat China." Representative Ross Rizley (Rep.-Okla.) commented, "I don't know anybody in the country who wants to go to war over aggression in the Far East. As for fighting over Thailand, most people don't even know where it is."

There were some last-minute discussion of the oncoming conflict. The *Chicago Tribune* conceded that U.S. bombers could destroy the populous Japanese cities, for their flimsy construction would invite disaster, but remarked that some Americans would not find this act the noblest work of their military. Borchard went even further, predicting that Japan might actually win a war, as its enemies would be preoccupied in a fight against Hitler.

Pearl Harbor. On December 7, 1941, the Japanese attacked the American base at Pearl Harbor, a strike that cost the United States the lives of 2,323 men and practically every airplane on Oahu. All eight battleships were disabled, two destroyed.

In private some anti-interventionists blamed the United States. Herbert Hoover claimed that Hull realized that his ultimatum of November 26 meant war. Charles A. Lindbergh commented, "We have been prodding them [the Japanese] for weeks." To General Wood, Roosevelt had finally gotten America into war through the back door. In public statements, the pacifist Fellowship of Reconciliation denied that ultimate war guilt rested with Japan alone for the United States too had acted provocatively. The *Christian Century* spoke of the war as an "unnecessary necessity."

Within four days after the Japanese strike, Hitler declared war on the United States. The two-front war that anti-interventionists had particularly dreaded was a reality. The National Council for the Prevention of War and the Women's International League hoped that a negotiated peace might come. The Fellowship of Reconciliation put much of its effort on protecting the rights of conscientious objectors. The Keep America Out of War Congress transformed itself into the Provisional Committee Towards a Democratic Peace, which in time became the Post-War World Council.

On the very day that Hitler declared war, the America First Committee disbanded. It made no apologies over its activities. Instead, in its closing statement, the AFC national committee said, "Our principles were right. Had they been followed, war could have been avoided." Yet, except for a handful of pacifists, Senator Wheeler gave the last word: "The only thing now is to do our best to lick hell out of them."

PART II

DOCUMENTS

DOCUMENT NO. 1

SENATOR WILLIAM E. BORAH
OPPOSES CASH AND CARRY [*]

During the 1920s Senator Borah could exert more influence than the secretary of state. Borah was a member of the Senate from 1907 until his death in 1940 and chaired its Foreign Relations Committee from 1924 to 1933. A gifted orator, adroit in argument but courteous in manner, Borah was a staunch progressive, favoring such reforms as prohibition, old-age pensions, and the abolition of child labor and wage discrimination against women. In fact, on domestic issues he was more supportive of Franklin D. Roosevelt than of any president since Franklin's kinsman Theodore. A staunch anti-interventionist by 1919, he opposed U.S. membership in the League of Nations and the World Court. At the same time, he endorsed the Washington Naval Conference of 1921–1922, the Kellogg-Briand Pact, independence for China, American recognition of the Soviet Union, and U.S. intervention in the Caribbean. In this reading, Borah saw the current European struggles as simply another chapter in the age-old search for the balance of power.

γ   γ   γ

We all know the feeling in this country against Germany, and I think we know that if it were not for that feeling we would not be here in session. However, the question with me is not my feeling against Germany, or my abhorrence of the cruel and brutal creed which is practiced in that nation. My desire is to permit nothing, whatever it may be, to lead me into a course which would bring my Nation into the conflict in Europe. . . .

For myself, and for myself only, I want to declare I look upon the present war in Europe as nothing more than another chapter in the bloody volume of European power politics, the balance of power which John Bright, the great commoner of England, once declared was the curse of any possible European peace. Yes; it is power politics.

It is the old question of the balance of power. Was it anything more than the balance of power when the democracies and the dictators of Europe in blessed accord stood over the dismembered body of Czecho-

[*]*Congressional Record*, October 2, 1939, pp. 71, 73–74.

slovakia, the only real republic in that portion of the world? Was it anything but power politics, the balance of power, when the Premier of Great Britain, holding aloft an agreement of settlement between the Premier of Great Britain and the Chancellor of Germany, told the people of Great Britain and all the world that there was peace, and peace with honor; that the master of Germany could be trusted?

Territorial settlements: Was the cruel and brutal and revolting creed of nazi-ism any different at Munich than it was at Warsaw? Was civilization and democracy any less under challenge when Czechoslovakia fell at the hands of the combined assassins than when Poland was threatened? Was it anything but power politics when Germany and Great Britain excluded Russia from the Munich conference, but both sought industriously to secure her aid, notwithstanding her creed, in the controversy relative to Poland? When the men at Munich reached the consummation of their awful deed, did they not turn over to the unlimited control and tender mercies thousands of a race whose presence excites the mortal wrath and vengeance of the one to whose control they assigned them? Was that humanity? Was that civilization? Was it saving democracy? Was it saving civilization? No; it was dividing territory. It was power politics. It was imperialism. . . .

What is going on now in Europe? Is it anything more than a controversy over territory, over power? We are being asked to approach and come nearer, step by step, to just such wars as have gone on in Europe from the Spanish succession to the present hour. . . .

A few days ago I read the following description of a scene of battle after these instrumentalities had done their work. I quote:

> Chunks of human flesh were quivering on the branches of the trees. . . . A half dozen houses were burning. . . . Mules and horses were pawing in their own entrails. . . . The whitewashed church was bespattered with blood and brains. . . . Men were running about howling with insanity, their eyes protruding from their sockets. . . . One woman was sitting against a wall trying to push her bleeding intestines back into her abdomen. . . . A man lay nearby, digging his teeth and his fingers into the ground. . . . A child sat on a doorstep whimperingly holding up the bleeding stumps of its arms to a dead woman whose face was missing.

Looking upon a scene as this, who would undertake to discriminate, to distinguish, between the manufacturer of the instruments which could produce such a scene, the purchaser, paper title or no paper titles, and legal technicalities? Let us stay out of this war. It is not our war.

DOCUMENT NO. 2

DALTON TRUMBO,
JOHNNY GOT HIS GUN (1939)*

Screen writer and novelist, Trumbo was strongly leftist in sympathy, joining the Communist party in 1943. From 1939 to 1941, when the Molotov-Ribbentrop Pact existed, Trumbo was vehemently anti-interventionist, even contributing to the conservative Chicago Tribune. Johnny Got His Gun *was a bitter antiwar account, popular enough to be the subject of a favorable editorial in the* New York Daily News, *which called it "a horror tale that outdoes anything of Edgar Allan Poe that we've ever seen." In 1971 the novel became a film, the studio using Trumbo's script. The book title came from the opening lines of Irving Berlin's patriotic song of World War I, "Over There": "Johnny, get your gun, get your gun, get your gun." This excerpt shows the disillusion of a combat veteran who has lost all faculties but his mind.*

γ   γ   γ

They were always fighting for something the bastards and if anyone dared say the hell with fighting it's all the same each war is like the other and nobody gets any good out of it why they hollered coward. If they weren't fighting for liberty they were fighting for independence or democracy or freedom or decency or honor or their native land or something else that didn't mean anything. The war was to make the world safe for democracy for the little countries for everybody. If the war was over now then the world must be all safe for democracy. Was it? And what kind of democracy? And how much? And whose?

Then there was this freedom the little guys were always getting killed for. Was it freedom from another country? Freedom from work or disease or death? Freedom from your mother-in-law? Please mister give us a bill of sale on this freedom before we go out and get killed. Give us a bill of sale drawn up plainly so we know in advance what we're getting killed for and give us also a first mortgage on something as security so we can be sure after we've won your war that we've got the same kind of freedom we bargained for.

And take decency. Everybody said America was fighting a war for the triumph of decency. But whose idea of decency? And decency for who? Speak up and tell us what decency is. Tell us how much better a decent dead man feels than an indecent live one. Make a comparison there in facts like houses and tables. Make it in words we can understand. And don't talk about honor. The honor of a Chinese or an Englishman or an African negro or an American or a Mexican? Please all you guys who want to fight to preserve our honor let us know what the hell honor is. Is it American honor for the whole world we're fighting for? Maybe the world doesn't like it. Maybe the South Sea Islanders like their honor better.

For Christ sake give us things to fight for we can see and feel and pin down and understand. No more highfalutin words that mean nothing like native land. Motherland fatherland homeland native land. It's all the same. What the hell good to you is your native land after you're dead? Whose native land is it after you're dead? If you get killed fighting for your native land you've bought a pig in a poke. You've paid for something you'll never collect.

· · · ·

You can always hear the people who are willing to sacrifice somebody else's life. They're plenty loud and they talk all the time. You can find them in churches and schools and newspapers and legislatures and congresses. That's their business. They sound wonderful. Death before dishonor. This ground sanctified by blood. These men who died so gloriously. They shall not have died in vain. Our noble dead.

Hmmmm.

But what do the dead say?

Did anybody ever come back from the dead any single one of the millions who got killed did any one of them ever come back and say by god I'm glad I'm dead because death is always better than dishonor? Did they say I'm glad I died to make the world safe for democracy? Did they say I like death better than losing liberty? Did any of them ever say it's good to think I got my guts blown out for the honor of my country? Did any of them ever say look at me I'm dead but I died for decency and that's better than being alive? Did any of them ever say here I am I've been rotting for two years in a foreign grave but it's wonderful to die for your native land? Did any of them say hurray I died for womanhood and I'm happy see how I sing even though my mouth is choked with worms?

. . . .

There's nothing noble about dying. Not even if you die for honor. Not even if you die the greatest hero the world ever saw. Not even if you're so great your name will never be forgotten and who's that great? The most important thing is your life little guys. You're worth nothing dead except for speeches. Don't let them kid you any more. Pay no attention when they tap you on the shoulder and say come along we've got to fight for liberty or whatever their word is there's always a word.

Just say mister I'm sorry I got no time to die I'm too busy and then turn and run like hell. If they say coward why don't pay any attention because it's your job to live not to die. If they talk about dying for principles that are bigger than life you say mister you're a liar. Nothing is bigger than life. There's nothing noble in death. What's noble about lying in the ground and rotting? What's noble about never seeing the sunshine again? What's noble about having your legs and arms blown off? What's noble about being an idiot? What's noble about being blind and deaf and dumb? What's noble about being dead? Because when you're dead mister it's all over. It's the end. You're less than a dog less than a rat less than a bee or an ant less than a little white maggot crawling around on a dungheap. You're dead mister and you died for nothing.

You're a dead mister.

Dead. . . .

DOCUMENT NO. 3

HOWARD K. BEALE, "SOME FALLACIES OF THE INTERVENTIONIST VIEW"*

In 1941, at the time Beale's pamphlet was published, he was on the faculty of the University of North Carolina and best known for his work on Andrew Johnson's presidency and on academic freedom. An ardent reformer, Beale was active in the American Civil Liberties Union and the National Association for the Advancement of Colored People. In this reading Beale shows how a convinced pacifist could analyze the war in terms of underlying forces.

γ γ γ

2. *That ideas can be defeated or established by defeat or victory on the battlefield.* In the days of the French Revolution the combined powers of Europe overwhelmingly defeated the French armies and in a few years the ideas of the French Revolution had spread all over Europe. The North overwhelmingly defeated the South's soldiers and sent armies of occupation to impose Northern ideas upon her and to "police" her, and the only effect was to heighten the determination of Southerners not to accept Northern ideas. Victories are not won for ideas by military successes. If nazism spreads permanently over the world it will be because in peacetime services to its people it succeeds well enough in Germany that other nations wish to adopt it or because, through war, we create conditions in America that make nazism seem desirable for the same reasons that it seemed desirable to Germans when they adopted it. If democracy is saved in the world it will be because by staying out of war America will be able to turn her vast energies to making democracy work so well in America that unhappy peoples elsewhere will wish to live under the system that is making Americans happy.

3. *That Germans are different from other people, like to be ordered about, enjoy being ruled by a tyrant, and take pleasure in war and destruction of their neighbors.* The Germans actually are much like any other people.

*From Howard K. Beale, "Some Fallacies of the Interventionist View" (pamphlet; privately printed, 1941), pp. 10–11, 13–14, 15.

A group of young Germans followed Hitler and accepted his teachings because conditions in Germany became so hopeless that thousands of young men who had never been able to get a job or to marry or live normal lives despaired of the future, and despair breeds phenomena like Hitler. But the great majority of Germans are human beings just like any of the rest of us who want to live and let live, to marry, have children, and feel safe in simple pleasures and in their old age. Outside of England there is no place in the world where Americans would feel so much at home as among the Germans of the Rhineland or the South of Germany. Actually the Germans are fighting as others are fighting and as we are asked to fight, because they are afraid, afraid in the early thirties of the encirclement they felt before they rearmed and afraid now of the consequences of stopping fighting in a war of which they like the rest of us are thoroughly sick.

5. *That Hitler was chiefly responsible for this war.* Anyone who knows the history of the western world between 1919 and 1933 should know this is not true. There was the Treaty of Versailles. Worse still there were the actions of the Allies in the years following when they were strong enough to treat a militarily weak Germany as they would. Important among the causes of the war were: the Allied starvation of Germany by blockade long after the war had ceased; the French invasion of the Ruhr; the refusal to allow Austria to join Germany by peaceful legal means under the very principles of self-determination that an American had so eloquently voiced; the failure of Allied democracies to help a German democracy to succeed; German despair induced by reparations whose end the grandchildren of living Germans could not foresee; failure to use the League of Nations peacefully to solve the disarmament problem, to rectify injustices, and to remove the economic problems such as widespread depression that made another war probable; failure of America to assume her responsibilities in the League in making the League work toward justice for all peoples; and humiliations and irritations of all sorts needlessly heaped upon Germans who could not resist them because they were forcibly disarmed.

. . . .

Allied democracies refused to grant the most just concessions to a German democracy. The Allies well taught Germany the lesson in those years that she could get a hearing and the granting of what she considered her rights in a world controlled by democracies for "democracy" under the international machinery of a society of nations only by reobtaining armed might sufficient to seize these rights by military force. This is what persuaded Germans to follow Hitler and brought a German people sick of war back to war as preferable to the peace they had got.

DOCUMENT NO. 4

EDWIN M. BORCHARD ON NEUTRALITY[*]

Professor at Yale University Law School from 1917 to 1950, Borchard was a staunch disciple of jurist John Bassett Moore, from whom he inherited an intense belief in traditional international law and an equally intense hatred of collective security. Borchard claimed that international law, as it existed before World War I, protected nations from "purposeless" involvement, permitted commercial prosperity, limited the scope of the fighting, and allowed for neutral mediation. After the war, he believed, well-established legal principles were replaced by foolish efforts to freeze the status quo and punish "aggressors," measures that only served to widen all conflicts and perpetuate continued chaos overseas. This selection shows how Borchard applied his general analysis to the conflict of 1939.

ɣ   ɣ   ɣ

The arms embargo has become something of a battlefield for these conflicting views of national policy. But before tracing the legislative struggle, it may be well to point out that the Geneva theory of combined action to punish and coerce "aggressors" came into head-on collision with both the theory and the practice of neutrality. It contemplated that when any country revolted against the established system—and at that time the one of Versailles seemed the desirable one to maintain—it would be denounced by all its associates as an aggressor and the combined use or threat of force would restore the revolter to order. This was supposed to insure peace, and the device became known by the reassuring term "collective security" or "sanctions" to "enforce peace."

The idea rested upon certain assumptions, namely, that the nations had arrived at relative stability, that the world represented primarily a moral order, that the coercers would remain united, that their interests and desires for peace would remain uniform, that the recalcitrant, endowed with the somewhat scurrilous name of aggressor—a concept elusive and altogether subjective—would surrender before a show of force or in contrition would cease and desist. It was assumed that nations

[*]From Edwin Borchard, speech to American Academy of Political and Social Science, Philadelphia, October 14, 1939, entered into Appendix, *Congressional Record*, October 21, 1939, pp. A415–416, 417.

judge each other objectively and not in the light of their interests, their alliances, and their prior commitments; that a country can be guaranteed against the consequences of its own ineptitude and against deterioration of its resources, physical and spiritual.

Every one of these assumptions involved delusions of the first magnitude, both historical and psychological, and every attempt to apply the system produced disorders which have been a material factor in the world's disorganization. This false mechanistic view of a dynamic world of living beings produced the strange thesis that the 90 percent of the peace-loving peoples should quarantine the warlike 10 percent. It is no wonder that these illusions as to how to enforce stability, purveyed to a disordered and essentially unmaintainable post-war world, helped to bring about an astronomical increase in armaments. The theory of combined coercion against aggressors had no roots in human experience and had to meet the fate that usually awaits unsound experiments.

But the most dangerous effects of this false theory were reserved for the United States. Neutrality, a national tradition, became the object of violent and unreasoning attack. And this is not unnatural, for if under the theory of sanctions everyone must join the posse comitatus against an aggressor, neutrality is necessarily taboo. The wisdom, the propriety, and the possibility of America's staying out of foreign wars were derided. The American principle of nonintervention was denounced as cowardly and immoral. . . .

If military help to the Allies is the motive—and the motive in these matters is all important—then the lifting of the embargo is an act of intervention, and it should be debated as such.

Many neutral countries have imposed arms embargoes during war. And it was always understood as a safeguard or insurance of its neutrality. To say that the lifting of an existing arms embargo is calculated to safeguard neutrality is unprecedented.

Moreover, the assumption that a neutral can change his law so as to help one side defeat the other and yet escape the consequences of war is hazardous. The gamble may be successful, but it is very speculative, for success depends on the inability or unwillingness of the disfavored belligerent to exert the reprisals which he would naturally wish to, and which he is privileged to exert. There may be good reasons why many Americans would like to help the Allies win this European war, but the public should not delude itself into the belief that a hostile act is a contribution to American neutrality.

The suggestion that the present act is unneutral, and hence must be corrected because Great Britain cannot legally secure the arms which Germany could not physically obtain is inaccurate and unsound. It would be more true to say that the naval position of the belligerents enables the United States to supply one side only with everything but arms. There is a practical embargo on Germany. This ought to satisfy the craving for discrimination, and it probably can be defended as legal. The lifting of the arms embargo, I fear, cannot be so defended.

It is proper to say that there are many arguments against an arms embargo. International law does not require a neutral to impose an arms embargo, although many neutrals in the course of history have done so. In the abstract, on historic evidence of the effects of general embargoes, I have been opposed to embargoes and boycotts in any form. And when applied discriminatorily, as so many Americans have been taught to believe was justified, they are particularly obnoxious. They constitute one of the most disturbing political instruments of an age that has been extraordinarily fertile in inventing new devices for provoking conflicts among people. But the arms embargo now under discussion is a special embargo enacted for a particular American purpose. To lift it now, after the outbreak of war, would be an illegal act of intervention. . . .

It is not true to say that a neutral may not change the rules of law during war. It is during war that most of the rules of neutrality were made. But the rules may only be changed in the direction of insuring and tightening neutral duties, and not in the direction of relaxing them for the benefit of one set of belligerents. This is a hostile act, and its consequences must be carefully weighed. It is inconsistent with that neutrality which official groups profess to wish to maintain.

DOCUMENT NO. 5

CHARLES A. LINDBERGH
ON BRITISH PROPAGANDA*

Because of his solo flight across the Atlantic in 1927, Lindbergh became the hero par excellence of the jaded generation of the twenties. From 1935 until 1939, he and his family lived in Europe, where he made intelligence estimates of German strength at the request of the U.S. military attaché in Berlin. More militant than many anti-interventionists, Lindbergh publicly expressed the hope that neither Britain nor Germany would win. In this selection, published in an interventionist weekly, "the Lone Eagle"—as he was called—claimed that interventionists had continually and dangerously distorted the military realities concerning the conflict.

γ   γ   γ

British propaganda in the United States attempts to persuade us that Great Britain will win the war, provided she receives somewhat more help than we have, up to this moment, given her. Coupled with this has been a campaign to convince us that a British victory is essential to American security. It is taken for granted that we would not be willing to take part in a war which we felt would be unsuccessful. Consequently, news releases from London minimize all German successes and exaggerate all British successes. They avoid any discussion of war aims, peace terms, or how England can win now that Germany has defeated France and controls the continent of Europe. This is simply the A B C of wartime propaganda. It is carried on by both sides in a war. I am discussing British propaganda because it is that to which we have been subjected and therein lies the danger of our involvement. There is certainly no danger of our fighting on Germany's side, and her propaganda in America has been relatively ineffective.

To be specific again, you will remember that even before hostilities commenced, factual statements concerning the growing military strength of Germany were bitterly attacked by the pro-British press. Those of us who saw the growth of the German air force were severely

---

*From Charles A. Lindbergh, "A Letter to Americans," *Collier's*, March 29, 1941, in Appendix, *Congressional Record*, entered March 24, 1941, p. A1404.

assailed because of the reports we made describing it, although these reports now turn out to have been almost unforgivably conservative. Then, you recall that when the Germans invaded Austria, it was claimed by the propagandists that their mechanized divisions broke down; that the workmanship on their tanks, trucks, engines, etc., was too inferior to operate successfully in a major war. German aircraft were said to be weakly constructed; there was a shortage of pilots, raw materials, and fuel. We were told that Germany did not have sufficient food to wage a war. And in addition to all this, internal conditions were said to be so bad that the German people would start a revolution rather than fight again.

If you question the accuracy of my statement that we have been misinformed through propaganda, I ask you to glance through our daily newspapers since the war began. If you are pressed for time, take any one of the major campaigns—Poland, Finland, Norway, Holland, Belgium, and France. You will find that we in America were misinformed about these campaigns until the actual military position made it impossible to hide the facts any longer. Do you remember when we were informed over the radio that the French Army had penetrated the Siegfried line in five different places? Do you recall the headlines of battles raging on the western front during the winter of 1939–40—battles we now know were never fought? Were we told how desperate the Finnish position was before the final break-through of the Russian Army? Do you remember how, after reading day after day of allied successes in Norway, and how Germany had put her neck in a noose, we were startled by the announcement that the Allies were evacuating all of their forces? Who was it said the Maginot line was impregnable; that bombing planes were no match for the British Navy; that England had the submarine menace well in hand and had already "won the battle of the air"?

DOCUMENT NO. 6

HARRY ELMER BARNES
ON "OLD" AND "NEW THIEVES"*

In 1940 Barnes was best known among historians for his book The Genesis of the World War *(1926),* in which he found responsibility for the outbreak of World War I lying far more with the Entente, particularly Russia and France, than with the Central Powers. A prolific author, Barnes in his lifetime wrote over thirty books, a hundred essays, and six hundred book reviews, in the process accumulating close to a hundred lines in* Who's Who in America. *Though increasingly seen today as a "Holocaust revisionist," in the early 1940s—and often thereafter—Barnes crusaded for a variety of liberal causes, including compulsory health insurance, abolition of the death penalty, and greater equality for women and blacks. Here he gives vent to a disillusionment shared by many liberals.*

γ   γ   γ

It may have been a great mistake for the American colonies to have left the British Empire in 1776, but that decision was not in the hands of this generation. Being out of the Empire, it may be wisest to conduct our foreign policy in the light of this fundamental historical reality. It is perfectly obvious that a pro-American approach to world affairs today is an extremely quaint attitude, but it may prove a healthy variation from the run-of-the-mill discussions. It is certainly not yet a treasonable way of looking at things, though it probably will be shortly after election day. We may well take advantage of the precious interval.

In clarifying the rôle of the United States in the world situation today it is desirable at the outset to dispel some of the more common myths which befog and distort our vision. Among these the following are the most important:

(1) This is a holy war with all the nice people on one side and all the murderers, idiots, thieves, liars, and degenerates on the other.

(2) We are certain to be invaded and overrun by a victorious coalition

*From Harry Elmer Barnes, "Europe's War and America's Democracy," *Virginia Quarterly Review* 16 (October 1940): 552–554. Reprinted with permission of *Virginia Quarterly Review*.

of Nazis, Fascists, and Stalinists after they have joined forces and conquered Europe, Asia, Australia, New Zealand, Polynesia, Madagascar, Africa, South America, Central America, the West Indies, and Mexico.

(3) The British navy always has been and is now our chief line of defense against every conceivable foreign enemy. If Britain is defeated we shall be utterly at the mercy of any country that looks upon us with an envious eye.

(4) It would be an unspeakable calamity for Germany to win and for Britain to lose in the present conflict.

Just who the nice people and who the world-villains are is and always has been a very debatable question. In this matter it is preëminently true that there is no accounting for tastes. My own preferences are for the French, but I would have difficulty in defending this prejudice on any ground other than my infantile conditioning. For a half century after the Civil War most literate Americans thought the Germans were the nicest people in the world and John Fiske used to tell us that the first great battle in American history was the battle of the Teutoburg Forest where stout Arminius destroyed the legions of Augustus. All our democracy was traced to the German backwoods. Just now it is somewhat of an understatement to say that we prize the British more highly than we do the Germans. But so did the French on June first of the present year. . . .

When it comes to such things as political treachery, diplomatic lying, wartime and imperialistic atrocities, territorial ambitions, and the like, no country or coalition of states enjoys any monopoly of good or evil. One can assemble a most shocking anthology from the historical records of Russia, Germany, Austria, France, Britain, Italy, or Spain. Indeed, our own record hardly warrants Mr. Hull's assumption that we can qualify readily to act as the moral schoolmaster of the world. The present war started out as a struggle of the Old Thieves against the New Thieves, in which the Old Thieves had the better manners and the New Thieves the better case, accepting as our scale of values those which prevail in an era of nationalism and capitalistic imperialism.

There is little probability that the totalitarians of the Old World will swoop down upon us after they have overcome and occupied all of the other land masses of the planet. They are far more likely to fight among themselves. Even if they do not, it is improbable that they will jeopardize the vast spoils of the Old World in order to launch a desperate venture in the Western Hemisphere. The totalitarian leaders may be knaves, but they are not fools. They will hold what they have gained in the Old World, and it will take them generations to organize and digest the spoils of victory. Save for the vaporings of disgruntled renegades and sensational journalists there is no evidence that the totalitarians even remotely contemplate any onslaught against us.

Having some knowledge of American history I cannot take too seriously the common allegation that the British navy has been our invariable and sole defense against a hostile and bellicose world. The British navy was hardly our first line of defense in 1776, 1808, 1812, 1862, or 1914. It might be well to ask, quite simply, just whom the British navy has ever protected us from. We have never been attacked or threatened by any powers save Britain and France.

In fact, it is not unfair to suggest that the British Empire is probably the chief menace to the peace of this country. It is not likely that the British will ever attack us in the future, but there is every probability that we will be dragged into any major war in which the British Empire is involved. If we must fight, it might be a healthy change for us to have one good war in self-defense.

Any friend of the democratic way of life will frankly concede that it would be a shocking thing for Germany to triumph in the Old World and to dominate all Europe west of Russia. But it is rather too late for the United States to do anything about that now. If we intervene at the present stage we would in all probability have to fight a totalitarian coalition dominating the Old World from the French Channel ports to the islands of Japan. In such a case, we could certainly not save Britain and we would be likely to meet an ignominious defeat in the bargain. The British did not welcome any proposals of American aid against Hitler or Japan when both could have been easily overcome. There is less than any reason for us to wreck American civilization in the futile effort to bail out the British Empire at the present writing.

DOCUMENT NO. 7

JOHN HAYNES HOLMES ON IMPERIALIST WAR[*]

As minister of New York City's Community Church from 1907 to 1949, Holmes epitomized the social gospel movement so pronounced in the Progressive era. Holmes was a strong Socialist, who continually backed Norman Thomas's bids for the presidency. Furthermore, he was a staunch follower of Mahatma Gandhi, even refusing to support the American war effort after the Japanese attacked Pearl Harbor. In this article, which appeared in the pacifist-leaning weekly Christian Century, *Holmes makes his anti-interventionist case of pragmatic grounds rather than those of an absolutist religious ethic.*

γ   γ   γ

First, then, as regards this present war. If America goes in will I support my country? No!—because, like Lytton Strachey in the last war, I don't believe in this war, which is only the latest of a long series of European conflicts rooted in the age-old struggle for military predominance and imperialistic rule. It was begun, years ago, in a rivalry between the old British empire and the new German reich which threatened for a time to resolve itself into an armed alliance between London and Berlin for the division of the world instead of into the present conflict for its universal mastery. It will end either in an improbable early peace, in which Britain and Germany will share the globe between them and perhaps make war on Russia, or in a remote collapse dictated by mutual exhaustion, in which, as in the case of the Peloponnesian War between Athens, the great sea-power of its day, and Sparta, the great land-power, the light of civilization will be extinguished.

If America goes into the war, it will be not for idealistic reasons but to serve her own imperialistic interests so closely identified with those of Britain, and to no result other than that of prolonging the duration and extending the range of a struggle in which her ruin will be added to the sum total of the ruin of mankind. There are elements of better

[*]From John Haynes Holmes, "If America is Drawn into the War," *Christian Century* 57 (December 11, 1940): 1547–1548; copyright 1941 Christian Century Foundation. Reprinted by permission from the December 11, 1940 issue of *The Christian Century*.

and worse in this war as in all human affairs. I prefer Churchill to Hitler, to put it mildly, just as in the Peloponnesian War I trust I would have preferred Pericles to Archidamus. But no one of these moral elements today in Europe, any more than in Greece yesterday, alters the nature of the event, which is the fundamentally immoral clash of competing imperialisms. In such an event, as Muriel Lester [prominent British pacifist] has reminded us, "it is not worse to covet empire than to cleave to empire."

. . . .

Unless and until America goes into it, I will labor to keep this country, the melting-pot of nations, outside of and above the battle, that she may use her compassionate and insistent influence as the pope declared, on the first anniversary of the war, he had used the influence of the Vatican, "for the reconciliation of peoples, to limit the extent of the conflict, to safeguard those who are in danger of being dragged in, and to alleviate the suffering that every war brings with it." If and when my country enters the war, I will join neither hand nor heart to the hostilities of the hour, but toil still for brotherhood, in love of friends and enemies alike, and for that peace which can alone save mankind from death.

Yes—and let Hitler run roughshod over the earth to triumph?

I should be the most disturbed by this easy challenge if I saw Hitler with the eyes of so many of my contemporaries—as a unique embodiment of wickedness, a monster intruded upon the earth like Satan come from hell. But I do not see him in this guise. I think it unscientific to isolate a man from the time and place which have together spawned him. To me Hitler is all that is horrible, but as such he is the product of our world, the veritable incarnation of our nationalistic, capitalistic and militaristic era. Whatever is worst in our civilization seems to have come to a vile head in him. He is our own sins sprung to life, to confound us, scourge us and perhaps destroy us.

It is remarkable that Hitler has done nothing not already familiar to us from direful example. Thus, he did not begin the persecution of the Jews, which has been a Christian practice for well-nigh two millennia. He did not originate the myth of race superiority, which has flourished for generations in this country in the relations of whites with blacks. He did not inaugurate the concentration camp, which the Spaniards imposed upon the Cubans, the English upon the Boers, and the Americans upon the Filipinos. He did not initiate the totalitarian state, which is only an extremity of tyranny as transmitted to our time by the Hapsburgs and the Romanovs. He did not invent the idea of the subjection of helpless peoples, as witness Britain in India, France in Morocco, and Belgium in the Congo. He did not even build his own military machine.

The very weapons that Hitler has developed so formidably and used so fearfully have come from other nations—the tank from Britain, the bomber from America and France, the machine gun and submarine from America. This man, so cruel, so ruthless, so revengeful, is not alien to ourselves. He is the perversion of our lusts, the poisoned distillation of our crimes. We would not be so aghast at his appearance did we not see in him, as in a glass darkly, the image of the world that we have made. Our sins have found us out, that's all. If Hitler triumphs, it will be as the punishment of our transgressions.

But will he triumph? He may, if we have no better manner of meeting him than with the weapons which he has so terribly turned against us. The resort to arms is no guarantee of victory. Even a predominance of arms in this struggle against the reich can insure only a prolonged process of mutual destruction, in which, to quote St. Augustine in his *The City of God*, "the conquerors are ever more like to the conquered than otherwise." This is what Mahatma Gandhi has in mind when he declares that he does "not want Britain to be defeated," nor yet "to be victorious in a trial of brute strength." "You want to kill nazism?" he asks. "You will never kill it by its indifferent adoption. You will have to be more ruthless than the nazis. To win the war, the British must adopt with greater thoroughness the same work of destruction as the Germans."

This would mark the real triumph of the nazis—the transformation of their foes into their own likeness by the sheer necessity of adopting nazi weapons, and nazi methods in the use of these weapons, as a means to victory. This is not the way to solve our problem, meet our danger, save our world. There must be a better way if all that is precious in human living is not by our own frenzy of fear to be doomed to the destruction now impending. Even though I could not find, or follow, this better way, I would not turn to what I know is as evil as it is disastrous.

DOCUMENT NO. 8

SENATOR GERALD P. NYE
ON BRITAIN AS "ACE AGGRESSOR"*

From 1925 to 1945, Nye served in the Senate, where he combined an agrarian radicalism on domestic policy with adherence to rigid neutrality in foreign relations. In 1935 he chaired the Senate's Special Committee Investigating the Munitions Industry, a post that made him one of the most famous legislators in the United States. In this selection he reveals the degree to which many of the most vocal anti-interventionists detested Britain and continually pointed to its imperialism.

γ   γ   γ

Shall we ally our country with Great Britain in the name of ending aggression upon this earth? That, it seems to me, is a rather immediate challenge growing out of our hatred of the aggressors and out of this pending lend-lease or throw-it-away bill.

BRITAIN THE ACE AGGRESSOR

If such an alliance for such a cause is to be our lot, then let it be acknowledged that our ally is the ace aggressor of all time. Britain's aggressions have filled the pages of history for centuries. Aggression has given Great Britain a third of the globe and brought into British subjugation hundreds of millions of peoples. Step by step through the centuries, and right down to the present time, British imperialism has extended British sovereignty over peoples until now the Empire numbers nearly if not all of a half billion souls. And these have been won by conquest, by invasion, by the very kind of aggression we deplore and want to stop today. Be honest; if we join Britain in the cause of stopping aggressors we join the power that has practiced more aggression than any power recorded in history. Honesty to ourselves and to those we represent requires us to review British aggression of the last 3 centuries.

Fear and hatred of aggressors has us about to do the very thing that will leave historians of another day bewildered when they come to account for our actions in these hours.

*Congressional Record, March 4, 1941, pp. 1722, 1730.

BRITAIN STILL TAKING TERRITORY

The British Empire is still taking territory when it wants it, whenever it gets the chance. It has grabbed territory so recently that even the encyclopedias have not been able to keep up with its latest aggression.

Mr. President, to prove the truth of this charge let me recite a little very recent history.

In 1937—that, as will be noticed, is only 4 years ago—at a time when the President of the United States and his followers were heatedly denouncing the "aggressor" nations, though I do not remember hearing them say anything about the British Empire, one of the most highhanded and unlawful pieces of international brigandage in recent history was taking place in southern Arabia. Who was the aggressor? Hitler? No one else, Mr. President, than the British Empire. . . .

Mr. President, I do not desire to appear cynical, but there are certain facts that ought to be borne in mind. In the first place, it is necessary to bear in mind that Mr. Churchill, who is now the head of the British Government, is and always has been one of the most pronounced imperialists in British public life.

CHURCHILL FOUGHT INDIAN CONCESSIONS

He has fought every grant of self-government, however small, to India. In a speech only a few weeks ago he went out of his way to deplore the fact that Irish ports are not now in the hands of the British Empire. He has given no pledge whatever that this war is not to be followed by further annexations of territory for the British Empire, just as the last World War was. On the contrary, Mr. President, today we see British troops occupying Iceland, Crete, Libya, pressing into Eritrea, into Italian Somaliland, into Ethiopia. We see those in control of vast portions of what has been the great French Empire announcing their adherence to General De Gaulle, who is financed by England, is supported by England, and is completely in the hands of England. General De Gaulle's so-called free French movement now claims to hold French Equatorial Africa, with more than 950,000 square miles of territory; the French Cameroons, with 166,000 square miles of territory; French possessions in India, Tahiti, New Caledonia, and the New Hebrides. Will these lands be given back to France after the war is over? No promises have been made, and no one can predict that these lands will be given back if France remains under the same government which is now in power in that country. As a matter of fact, Mr. President, in all these

occupations of territory which Great Britain has made since the outbreak of the present war, there is only one case in which she has given
specific promise that after the war is over she will give up the territory.
That is the case of Iceland. For some reason, no one seems very anxious
to grab the desolate stretches of that island washed by Arctic waves.

DOCUMENT NO. 9

GENERAL HUGH S. JOHNSON, "IS BRITAIN FIGHTING OUR WAR?"*

One of the most colorful of the anti-interventionists, Johnson saw all life as melodrama and was well known for his salty speech and fiery invective. As a captain on the army's legal staff, he wrote major sections of the 1917 Selective Service Act. In 1933 Roosevelt appointed Johnson director of the National Recovery Administration, initially the linchpin of the entire New Deal program, but the vituperative personality of "Old Ironpants" resulted in his resignation the following year. Here he attacks the claim that U.S. security was long dependent upon Britain's strength.

γ   γ   γ

If our peace and defense have depended and now depend on England and England is at bay, we ought to go to war with everything we have. Once again we ought to adopt a war dictatorship as our form of government and once again pour out the full measure of our blood and fortune on foreign shores to the shattering of our own domestic economy and the possible destruction of the nation we have known and loved.

Of course, it is nonsense to say that the British have defended us. As for the Monroe Doctrine, it has been seriously threatened only twice in its existence and England had something to do with both attempts— once in Venezuela when we threatened war and stopped her from seizing territory, and as an original party to landing European troops in Mexico when we were tied up with the Civil War. She is the only European nation that has actually taken additional American territory since Monroe, and in defiance of that doctrine, and she did it twice, once in Honduras, once in the Faulkland Islands.

For her own purposes England has commanded the seas, not only the Atlantic but all oceans; but setting her navy aside for a moment, there has never been a time in the past forty years when any other nation was in a naval position to challenge either our country or our Monroe Doctrine in the face of our own fleet.

*From General Hugh S. Johnson, "Defend America First," radio address of September 5, 1940, in *Vital Speeches* 6 (October 1, 1940): 764.

Now this is no time to rake up old wrongs against Britain, but in view of the arguments that are made to edge and jostle us into this war, it certainly is high time to explode all these old errors in this regard. Quite aside from all that, this country should have seen enough of what is going on in the world today to know that any nation which must rely for its own peace and its own defense on the strength of any other nation is lost. We can't rely on any other power but our own, Great Britain or any other. We can rely on nothing on this earth but the strength of our own right arm, our own resources, and the patriotism, valor and fidelity of our own people—and thanks be to God, it is enough.

DOCUMENT NO. 10

STUART CHASE, "FOUR ASSUMPTIONS ABOUT THE WAR"[*]

Of all the advocates of centralized national planning, few had the popular influence of Stuart Chase. By using simple terminology and concrete illustrations, Chase won many over to his crusades against waste in resources, polemics in political language, exploitation of consumers, and laissez-faire economics. This reading illustrates Chase's distinction between the potential of an independent New World and the encumbrances of the Old one.

ɣ   ɣ   ɣ

In the United States, citizens elect their leaders and have wide latitudes in the exercise of free speech, free press, free assembly, free worship, and freedom from being pushed around by autocrats, priests, land owners, gentlemen in colored shirts, and the secret police. They are not immune from being pushed around—witness the Negroes and the Okies—but relative to Old World citizens, they are free men. Even in Britain, Sweden, and Switzerland today one has to do what the authorities tell one to do, or else.

A major test of stability was the great depression of 1929, which presently caused Europe to fall apart, but only rocked without shattering the Americas. We have found a sound culture bed. From this base, rough as it is, great developments are clearly visible—the abolition of poverty, unprecedented improvements in health and energy, a towering renaissance in the arts; an architecture and an engineering to challenge the gods. Toward these ends we are groping, with firm ground under our feet. We are the New World. We are the hope of mankind. Our culture is not burdened with the terrible dead weights which the Old World must carry. . . .

The United States cannot solve the political and economic problems of Europe, Asia, Africa, and the Indies by armed assault on their totalitarian leaders. Consider what is involved. First, a military adventure—and we cannot possibly equip ourselves for military adventures overseas

---

[*]Stuart Chase, "Four Assumptions About the War," *Uncensored*, December 28, 1940, in Appendix, *Congressional Record*, entered January 10, 1941, pp. A82–83.

before 1944 at the earliest—in which America takes on Germany, Italy, and Japan with their smaller allies, and before the show is over perhaps Russia, Spain, and France as well. Britain might be more of a liability than an asset in this adventure because of the extreme vulnerability of the British Isles. Pledged to defend this outpost, now flanked by enemy bases and ringed on the west by fleets of submarines, we should be severly handicapped in our efforts to make a frontal assault on the European, African, or Asiatic mainland. If we confined our military effort solely to the defense of Britain, we might save the British Isles, and we might not. It would, I suspect, be a full-time job, and leave us little energy for the reduction of Berlin, Rome, Tokyo, Madrid, and Moscow.

On the fantastic assumption that all these capitals were in our hands, what then? Our work would have just begun. Then we should have to find a social framework to fit some 1,500,000,000 people, burdened with the cleavages just mentioned, and say to them: "Take this and like it." We can be quite sure that many of them, perhaps most of them, won't like it. So then we might try to make them like it. One way would be to keep a few million American boys, armed to the teeth, in constant attendance to see that they like it. Another would be concentration camps. Another would be puppet governments with strings pulled from Washington.

How long would this educational program take? How long should we be in establishing our new order in Europe, Asia, Africa, and the Indies? And what if the blueprint turned out to be no good? Would the pattern we impose fit the revolutionary changes that are already far gone in those parts? Whom, by the way, would you nominate to prepare the blueprints—Mr. Walter Lippmann [prominent columnist], Mr. Jesse Jones [director Reconstruction Finance Corporation], Mr. Hoover? When people say we ought to go and help Britain knock out Hitler and restore democracy, the free market, and the little nations, they apparently have no conception of what such a crusade entails. Their imaginations go riotously to the shooting of Hitler, and there they stop. I grant it is a satisfying picture, but unfortunately the removal of Hitler would be only a preliminary incident in the total task before us.

Americans are fine, upstanding, enterprising folks. They could probably organize and defend the whole Western Hemisphere by giving their entire attention to the job. Or they might possibly win a stalemate peace for Britain, which would preserve her shattered island and her honor. But I do not see how they can do what I have indicated above. Giving

Britain her island and her honor, furthermore, settles nothing, with Europe and Asia still in totalitarian hands.

DOMESTIC DANGER

If Americans attempt this program, whether they knock out the dictators or not, they will most assuredly wreck their own New World pattern. As I said, we are an enterprising people. When we start a thing we like to finish it. We have never lost a war yet. With war once declared, or acts of war committed, there would be no end except victory or defeat—unless it were the utter exhaustion of both sides.

The consequences to our culture of an all-out war abroad are simply told—M-Day [day of national mobilization], the liquidation of political democracy, of Congress, the Supreme Court, private enterprise, the banks, free press, and free speech; the persecution of German-Americans and Italian-Americans, witch hunts, forced labor, fixed prices, rationing, astronomical debts, and the rest. We would become as a people tough, cruel, and vindictive. Scientific research would go to pot. With the whole world on our hands, draining our lifeblood overseas, we would have no time and no desire to plan for the America of the future. Our pattern would be smashed beyond repair.

UNITED STATES POLICY

If these assumptions are valid, what should be the foreign policy of the United States?

1. Arm to the point where no Old World power or combination of powers will dare attack us.

2. Link the Western Hemisphere into a self-sufficient economic unit, pending the time when the peoples of the Old World have achieved a stability which warrants cooperation with them.

3. As a salute to a brave nation fighting against great odds, give Britain all the material aid we can spare from our defense requirements. The amount should be determined by technicians rather than politicians. Britain is not fighting our war. France was not fighting our war—neither were Holland, Belgium, Poland, Finland, or Norway. European nations are fighting because their continental pattern makes no sense. They will go on fighting in this war and in other wars until they learn how to live peaceably together. We have learned this lesson on our continent. Our war, if it comes, must be to defend what we have learned.

DOCUMENT NO. 11

CHARLES A. LINDBERGH ON AIR DEFENSE[*]

Lindbergh's emphasis on air power was shared by many anti-interventionists. Because, however, he was the most prominent aviator of his time, his words were given much authority. In this selection, a radio speech made just after the Germans entered Brussels, Lindbergh sought to deal with the circumstance that, in his words, "The conservative who scoffed at aviation yesterday has become the radical who says that tomorrow we will be invaded by European aircraft."

γ　　　　　γ　　　　　γ

Let us reexamine the position of America in the air. New discoveries and developments affect nations in different ways. In Europe aviation has affected England adversely and Germany advantageously. One nation may have a psychology and topography which promotes the development of aviation, while another finds itself entirely unadjusted to the tempo of the air.

UNITED STATES IN FORTUNATE POSITION

Judged by aeronautical standards, we in the United States are in a singularly fortunate position. Our people have natural ability in the design, construction, and operation of aircraft. Our highly organized industry, our widely separated centers of population, our elimination of formalities in interstate travel, all contribute to the development of American aviation. From the standpoint of defense, we still have two great oceans between us and the warring armies of Europe and Asia.

In fact, there is hardly a natural element contributing to air strength and impregnability that we do not now possess. Aviation is for us an asset. It adds to our national safety. With a firm and clear-cut policy, we can build an air defense for America that will stand above these shifting sands of war.

But until we have decided upon a definite policy of defense the mere construction of large numbers of aircraft will not be adequate for our national safety. In fact, without a strong policy of defense, we will not

[*]From Charles A. Lindbergh, radio address of May 19, 1940, in Appendix, *Congressional Record*, entered May 20, 1940, pp. 3034–3035.

even know what types of planes to build. The speed and range of our fighting planes must depend upon the bases available for their use.

If we are to defend the United States alone, then we must construct numerous air bases along the Mexican and Canadian borders. Such a plan would require numbers of small bombers and pursuit planes, and eventually it would leave us as vulnerable to air attack as the nations of Europe are today. On the other hand, if we are to defend the entire Western Hemisphere, we need long-range bombers capable of attacking a hostile fleet a thousand miles or more at sea. But there is little use discussing types and numbers until a defense policy is established.

OTHER NATIONS MUST AID

This bring us to an issue which must sooner or later be faced. An adequate air defense of the Western Hemisphere necessitates the cooperation of the other nations of this hemisphere. Our military aircraft must have access to their bases. Their foreign policy must have some relationship to ours. We cannot hold this hemisphere free from foreign war if nations which lie within it declare war on foreign powers.

Let us not be confused by this talk of invasion by European aircraft. The air defense of America is as simple as the attack is difficult when the true facts are faced. We are in danger of war today not because European people have attempted to interfere with the internal affairs of America, but because American people have attempted to interfere with the internal affairs of Europe.

It is true that bombing planes can be built with sufficient range to cross the Atlantic and return. They can be built either in America or Europe. Aeronautical engineers have known this for many years. But the cost is high, the target large, and the military effectiveness small. Such planes do not exist today in any air force. A foreign power could not conquer us by dropping bombs in this country unless the bombing were accompanied by an invading army. And an invading army requires thousands of small bombers and pursuit planes; it would have little use for huge trans-Atlantic aircraft.

No; the advantage lies with us, for great armies must still cross oceans by ship. Only relatively small forces can be transported by air today, and over distances of a few hundred miles at most. This has great significance in Europe, but it is not an element that we have to contend with in America.

Such a danger can come, in any predictable future, only through division and war among our own peoples. As long as American nations work together, as long as we maintain reasonable defense forces, there will be no invasion by foreign aircraft. And no foreign navy will dare to approach within bombing range of our coasts.

SEES INTERNAL DANGER

Our danger in America is an internal danger. We need not fear a foreign invasion unless American peoples bring it on through their own quarreling and meddling with affairs abroad. Our eyes should not search beyond the horizon for problems which lie at our feet. The greatest lesson we can draw from Europe today is that national strength must be built within a nation itself and cannot be achieved by limiting the strength of others.

What of the unforeseen developments of a science? Rocket propulsion? New forms of energy? New methods of destruction? No generation can entirely safeguard the future for those that follow. They must meet their own problems as those problems arise. The greatest inheritance we can pass on to our children is a reasonable solution of the problems that confront us in our time—a strong nation, a lack of debt, a solid American character free from the entanglements of the Old World.

Let us guard America today as our forefathers guarded it in the past. They won this country from Europe with a handful of Revolutionary soldiers. We certainly can hold it now with a population of 130,000,000 people. If we cannot, we are unworthy to have it.

DOCUMENT NO. 12

HANSON W. BALDWIN ON "THE BOGEY OF INVASION"[*]

A graduate of the United States Naval Academy, Baldwin served at sea for several years before becoming a reporter. Because of his interest in military affairs, he often covered naval, air, and army maneuvers. In 1937 he became military editor for the New York Times, *at which point he spent several months in Europe studying the defenses of the various powers. In this selection, he stresses American invulnerability, a claim often made by anti-interventionists.*

γ   γ   γ

The author does not know a single responsible military or naval officer or government official who believes that this nation is threatened by *direct* invasion, even if Germany wins. Consider the difficulties.

No potentially hostile European or Asiatic power possesses territory or bases in this hemisphere.

The Atlantic is 3,000 miles across; from 4,000 to 7,000 miles of Pacific waters intervene between the continental United States and Asia.

Invaders can reach this country only by ship or by plane; armies cannot swim to victory.

No single power except Britain has a navy equal to our own. No two other powers are building as many combat ships as we are. . . .

Our navy today is probably capable of meeting in its own waters the present combined fleets of Germany, Italy, Russia, and Japan. Our fleet is the world's only real blue-water navy. . . .

Today the totalitarian powers could muster against us a tenuous and theoretical superiority only if their own waters were entirely stripped of all naval protection and a weird conglomeration of ill-adjusted fighting ships sent from 3,000 to 5,000 miles across the seas on a mission for which they were never designed and never intended. Our own fleet, a tactical, unified whole, fighting in close proximity to its own bases, able to shift rapidly from ocean to ocean by the interior line of the Panama

[*]From *United We Stand! Defense of the Western Hemisphere* (New York: Whittlesey House, 1941), pp. 75–76, 77–79, 80.

Canal, aided by shore-based aircraft would have an insuperable advantage over a conglomeration of ships operating thousands of miles from bases and constantly subject to air and submarine attack. . . .

What of an army transported to these shores?

It cannot reach here by swimming; it cannot reach here by air; the only carrier with capacity enough to transport the soldiers and the stuff of war is the vulnerable cargo ship. If our defensive forces on sea and in the air were sufficiently alert no army could ever reach these shores. But let us suppose the fleet was disabled, occupied in the Pacific or otherwise out of action; let us suppose that an army was sent by sea to establish a beach head somewhere along the New Jersey coast. Consider the technical problems involved. Each soldier with his equipment requires at least six and a half tons of cargo space. If he is in a mechanized force he may require as high as fifteen tons. Troop transports are extremely vulnerable to submarine and destroyer attack; they must be assembled in convoys, carefully protected by warships. Fifty thousand troops—one-eighth of the number in our Regular Army—would require at least 350,000 tons of shipping, or from 45 to 55 ships. This is the largest possible force that could be handled initially.

These ships would have to be crammed full of all the stuff of war—soldiers, ammunition, special landing boats, field guns, anti-tank guns, planes, and tanks. A 155-mm. gun with carriage and limber weighs fifteen tons, and tanks from two to forty-five tons apiece. Special cargo handling gear would have to be rigged up to load and unload the considerable weights.

The transports, although screened by the fighting ships, are nevertheless vulnerable. They would be subject to torpedo attack from submarines, torpedo boats, and destroyers by day and by night as they approached our shores and hammered by bombs as they steamed within bombing range.

Nor could they steam to a dock and unload men and heavy equipment with the aid of dock facilities. Harbors and ports are defended by mines, protected by shore guns and planes. Neither British nor German vessels, although their bases are now only some twenty miles apart, dare to venture into the other's harbors.

The disembarkation and landing operation might well result in a far worse shambles than Gallipoli [World War I campaign, 1915–16]. Under fire from bomb and gun, soldiers and heavy equipment would have to be transshipped to small boats from the transports anchored off shore. Then the small boats would have to make a landing through the surf. Once on the hostile beach, the enemy would have to struggle to get their tanks and field pieces off ramp-bowed landing boats onto the beach under shells and machine-gun fire, their only support, their carrier-based aviation and the guns of their warships.

. . . .

Any attempted conquest of the United States seems foredoomed to failure unless the aggressor nations first establish advanced bases of considerable strength strategically located within the Western Hemisphere. Practically all military observers are agreed that without such bases attempted invasion of this nation would be foolhardy in the extreme. Without such bases enemy blows against us would have to be limited chiefly to a warfare of economic attrition or to sporadic raids which would be irritating but not militarily serious.

DOCUMENT NO. 13

SENATOR ROBERT A. TAFT
ON CONSCRIPTION INEQUITY*

Serving in the Senate from 1938 until his death in 1953, Taft was a highly articulate critic of New Deal domestic programs. Like Herbert Hoover, to whom he was always personally close, Taft was more moderate than many anti-interventionists and indeed spoke far less on this topic than such congressional wheelhorses as Wheeler, Fish, and Nye. His most ardent stance centered on opposition to the 1940 draft, and the following remarks to the Senate shows how he linked the conscription issue to two matters he always held dear—individual liberty and equality of opportunity.

γ   γ   γ

It is said that a compulsory draft is a democratic system. I deny that it has anything to do with democracy. It is neither democratic nor undemocratic. It is far more typical of totalitarian nations than of democratic nations. The theory behind it leads directly to totalitarianism. It is absolutely opposed to the principles of individual liberty which have always been considered a part of American democracy. To choose 1 man in 10 by lot, and require him to leave his home against his will, is more like roulette than it is like democracy. Many people came to this country for the single purpose of avoiding the requirements of military service in Europe. This country has always been opposed to a large standing army, and it has been opposed to the use of the draft except in time of war when it may be absolutely necessary. I shrink from the very setting up of thousands of draft boards, with clerks and employees, and endless paper work and red tape; from the registration of 12,000,000 men and the prying into every feature of their lives, their physical condition, their religious convictions, their financial status, and even their hobbies.
. . .

The draft is said to be democratic because it hits the rich as well as the poor. Since the rich are about 2 percent of the total, it is still true that 98 percent of those drafted are going to be the boys without means. In fact, it is probable that under the volunteer system you would get a

*Congressional Record, August 14, 1940, pp. 10302–10303.

greater percentage of wealthy boys than under the draft. These boys all go to college, and the percentage of enlistment from the colleges has always been higher, because the need for the defense of this country against countries thousands of miles distant is brought home to those in the colleges more forcibly than it is to the boy who is employed locally, and to whom international affairs are a great many thousand miles away.

The principle of a compulsory draft is basically wrong. If we must use compulsion to get an army, why not use compulsion to get men for other essential tasks? We must have men to manufacture munitions, implements of war, war vessels, and other equipment. Why not draft labor for these occupations at wages lower than the standard? There are many other industries absolutely essential to defense, like the utility industries, the railroads, the coal-mining industry. Why not draft men for those industries also at $21 a month? Protection is absolutely essential against domestic violence. If we draft soldiers, why not draft policemen and firemen for city and State service? The maintenance of an army on inadequate pay is merely a matter of precedent with no justification under our form of government. To a certain extent the draft act recognizes that the Government may compel men to remain in war industries, for they are exempted for that purpose, but told that if they leave that industry they must at once become subject to draft. The logical conclusion of this peacetime conscription bill is that we should draft all labor and assign all men to the jobs we think they ought to have.

DOCUMENT NO. 14

ST. LOUIS POST-DISPATCH ON
ROOSEVELT AS DICTATOR*

The St. Louis Post-Dispatch *was published by Joseph Pulitzer, Jr., a member of the famous newspaper family. Distinguished for its editorial courage and high journalistic standards, the paper supported much of the New Deal. This editorial hits Roosevelt about the destroyer-bases deal at one of his most vulnerable points, the stretching of executive power to what many later would call "the imperial presidency." One sign of the* Post-Dispatch's *fierce independence lies in the fact that shortly after the editorial was written, the paper backed FDR for a third term.*

γ   γ   γ

DICTATOR ROOSEVELT COMMITS AN ACT OF WAR

Mr. Roosevelt today committed an act of war.

He also became America's first dictator.

Secretly, his Secretary of State, Mr. Hull, entered into an agreement with the British Ambassador that amounts to a military and naval alliance with Great Britain. This secretly negotiated agreement was consummated yesterday, September 2.

Today Congress is informed of the agreement. Note well the word "informed." Although the President referred to his undercover deal as ranking in importance with the Louisiana Purchase, he is not asking Congress—the elected representatives of the people—to ratify this deal. He is telling them it already has been ratified by him—America's dictator.

The President has passed down an edict that compares with the edicts forced down the throats of Germans, Italians, and Russians by Hitler, Mussolini, and Stalin.

He hands down an edict that may eventually result in the shedding of the blood of millions of Americans; that may result in transforming the United States into a goose-stepping, regimented slave state.

Under our Constitution, treaties with foreign powers are not legal

*"Dictator Roosevelt Commits an Act of War," *St. Louis Post-Dispatch*, September 3, 1940, in *Congressional Record*, September 5, 1940, p. 11423.

without the advice and consent of the Senate. This treaty, which history may define as the most momentous one ever made in our history, was put over without asking the Senate either for its advice or its consent.

The authority which the President quotes for his fatal and secret deal is an opinion from the Attorney General. Whatever legal trickery this "yes man" may conjure up, the fact is that the transfer of the destroyers is not only in violation of American law, but is also in violation of the Hague covenant of 1907, solemnly ratified by the United States Senate in 1908. It is an outright act of war.

Undeterred by law or the most primitive form of common sense, the President is turning over to a warring power about one-seventh of the United States Navy, against the repeated statements of Senators, Navy Department officials, and officers of the Navy that the ships are needed for our own defense.

But that is only one phase of this insane performance. We get in exchange leases on British possessions in this hemisphere—but only leases. What good will these leases be if Hitler should acquire title to these islands by right of conquest? There is even the possibility that, in the course of a negotiated peace, Great Britain might be forced to cede these islands to Hitler.

What, then, will become of Roosevelt's leases? Obviously, to avoid all sorts of possible complications, we should have full sovereignty over our naval and air bases.

Of all "sucker" real-estate deals in history, this is the worst, and the President of the United States is the "sucker."

Thomas Jefferson did not lease Louisiana from Napoleon Bonaparte. He acquired it outright, to have and to hold forever.

Woodrow Wilson didn't lease the Virgin Islands from Denmark. With the advice and consent of the United States Senate, he bought them.

In the case of Newfoundland and Bermuda, Mr. Roosevelt tells us that the right to bases "are gifts—generously given and gladly received." In other words, the great and rich United States is taking largess from a nation that owes us some $4,000,000,000. We are accepting a tip, according to the President.

For at least 10 years, this newspaper has repeatedly called attention to the urgent desirability of acquiring Caribbean islands owned by Britain and France for our own defense purposes. In that belief, we are ardently in agreement with Mr. Roosevelt.

No move was made to this end by Roosevelt or his predecessors, despite the fact that we had a trading argument in the billions of war debts owed to us by France and Britain.

No. Roosevelt saw France go down without negotiating for the islands in exchange for the debts, and only now, with Britain in the throes of a desperate war, does the President move to protect our shores.

But, in doing so, he commits an act of war, he strips our Navy of 50 valuable ships, and he enters into leases which might not be worth the paper they are written upon in a month's time.

And all this is done in utmost contempt of democratic processes and the Constitution of the United States.

If this secret deal goes through, the fat is in the fire, and we all may as well get ready for a full-dress participation in the European war.

If Roosevelt gets away with this, we may as well say good-bye to our liberties and make up our mind that henceforth we live under a dictatorship.

If Congress and the people do not rise in solemn wrath to stop Roosevelt now—at this moment—then the country deserves the stupendous tragedy that looms right around the corner.

DOCUMENT NO. 15

GENERAL HUGH S. JOHNSON
ON DEFENDING AMERICA FIRST[*]

This radio address shows that the America First Committee had its origin in a dual anxiety: not only was the United States moving inexorably towards full-scale intervention in the war; it was denuding itself of weapons crucial to its survival.

γ   γ   γ

This country is united as never before on national defense. The people have been ahead of their leaders. The leaders let defense lag shamelessly. The people demanded action. The leaders hesitated to increase taxes for defense; the people insisted on total defense at any sacrifice.

We need waste no words arguing on unity for defense; it is now complete.

But there is a very great and dangerous difference of opinion on what national defense means.

There is a committee in this country called Defend America by Aiding the Allies. Since there are no longer any Allies that means defend America by defending England. There is another committee called Defend America First. That is my ticket.

The Defend England Committee announced yesterday that of England's two million man army, one-quarter of them, or 500,000, are armed with American army rifles, that 100,000 tons of arms and explosives have been taken from our defense and sent to Britain, 80 machine guns, 700 field artillery guns, mountains of ammunition, all shortage items with us.

This committee wants to send from our army its flying fortresses, tanks, 250,000 more rifles, and the marvelous American secret bombsight. It wants to use our flying fields to train pilots for Britain and thinks we ought to detach a lot more ships from our Navy.

The same day's news discloses that our own army has less than 300 first-line combat planes and only 59 heavy bombers. We have ordered

[*]From General Hugh S. Johnson, "Defend America First," radio address of September 5, 1940, in *Vital Speeches* 6 (October 1, 1940): 763–764.

only 1,500 modern fighting planes, only 176 heavy bombers—many of them won't be delivered for over a year. We have not enough modern equipment for an army of 100,000 men. We have not even, to use a famous weasel word, "on order" equipment for the number of men we now plan to conscript. I don't know just how much of this helplessness and delay is due to defending America by defending Britain, but I know that a lot of it is due to that alone.

AMERICA'S SYMPATHIES

There are very few Americans who do not hate Hitler and hope that Britain wins. Our sympathies are all with England, but modern war is not risked by any wise nation, as George Washington was careful to tell us, for any reason other than its own defense or some other absolutely compelling cause. That is the reason why our friends who want us to take part in this war call their committee Defend America and add "by Helping Britain."

They have gone a long distance with that slogan. Their argument is that our peace depends upon the British Navy. They go a lot further than that. They say that our peace, our Monroe Doctrine and the tranquility of the Americas always has depended on the British Navy. Therefore, they say Britain is fighting our war, Britain is fighting to defend us. We owe it, ought in gratitude in our own defense, to help Britain; so they want to strip our army, navy and air power of their ships and guns and ammunition and by various blind pig loopholes in our own statutes, our treaties and international law, bootleg these hundreds of thousands of tons of lethal weapons to England.

DOCUMENT NO. 16

CHARLES A. BEARD ON U.S. POLICY[*]

Without question Beard was one of the most noted, if not the most noted, American historian of this century. A prolific writer, he and his wife Mary Ritter Beard coauthored The Rise of American Civilization *(1927), deemed one of the most influential books of its time. Beard was a strong reformer who increasingly found the New Deal lacking rational planning. His anti-interventionism was rooted in the belief that the United States laid claim to being a distinct and unique civilization that had successfully repudiated the feudal institutions, class bitterness, and ethnic hatreds of the Old World. In this passage opposing lend-lease Beard warns against bestowing dictatorial power on the president and dissipating American strength in search of futile objectives.*

γ   γ   γ

It is in this spirit, I must beg you to believe, gentlemen of the committee, that I approach the issue before us. There is no question here of sympathy for Britain; this Nation is almost unanimous in its sympathy. There is no question here of aid to Britain; the Nation is agreed on that. Our immediate task is to analyze the meaning of the language employed in this bill, and to calculate as far as may be humanly possible the consequences for our country that are likely to flow from its enactment into law—to rend, if we can, some corner of the dark veil that hides the future from our vision.

By the definitions of section 2, every article or commodity, all resources and powers of production, which the President is pleased to regard as for defense, are placed unreservedly at his command. In other words, he may use and dispose of, as he likes, every machine, every tool, every ship, every industry, the labor of every able-bodied person, in any way that he deems desirable, under the loose, indeed limitless, phrase, "national defense."

In the midst of a declared war already raging, President Wilson called upon Congress for no such powers, no such surrender of its con-

[*]From Testimony, Senate Foreign Relations Committee, February 4, 1941, pp. 308–310, 311–312.

stitutional prerogatives. Even in the midst of a frightful civil war, testing whether this Nation could endure, President Lincoln demanded of Congress no such abject capitulation and humiliation.

There can be no doubt about this. The bill would subject all labor energies and all the wealth of the United States to the President's personal orders issued at his discretion. Only the lines of the poet Milton seem appropriate to describe such power:

Without dimension, where length, breadth, and height,
And time, and place are lost.

After the President has "procured" this wealth or any part of it, what may he do with it? The bill indicates some possible actions. It says that the President may "sell, transfer, exchange, lease, or lend" any part of it or all of it to any government whose defense he deems vital to the defense of the United States; that is, to any government he pleases so to designate.

That is not all. The President is not limited to selling, transferring, exchanging, or leasing the wealth of the United States or any part of it. Paragraph 2 of section 3 also provides that the President may "otherwise dispose of" this wealth or any part of it. Mark the words, "otherwise dispose of." If words mean anything, he may give it away and use the armed forces of the United States to carry it anywhere on terms which he alone may prescribe.

There is more involved. Paragraph 3 of section 3 gives the President power to repair, outfit, recondition, or otherwise place in good working order any war craft for any government which he is pleased to name as vital for the defense of the United States. If words mean anything, these words mean that the President can turn naval bases, shipyards, and harbors of the United States over to the business of repairing and outfitting vessels for belligerents named by his orders; that is, he can convert areas of the United States into areas of warfare and thus expose them to direct retaliation by other belligerents.

Given the sweeping language of this bill, it seems fitting to suggest that the title is imprecise. The title is—

An act to promote the defense of the United States.

It should read:

All provisions of law and the Constitution to the contrary notwithstanding, an Act to place all the wealth and all the men and women of the United States at the free disposal of the President, to permit him to transfer or carry goods to any foreign government he may be pleased to designate, anywhere in the world, to authorize him to wage undeclared wars for anybody, anywhere in the world, until the affairs of the world are ordered to suit his policies, and for any other purpose he may have in mind now or at any time in the future, which may be remotely related to the contingencies contemplated in the title of this Act.

I suggest that as a new title for the bill.

We come to the consequences likely to flow from this act. If the bill is not to be an empty gesture, the President will act under its provisions. First, he will begin, without any statutory or constitutional restraints worthy of mention, to draft the industries, labor, and resources of the United States under orders of his own formulation. Second, under paragraph 3, section 3, he will designate certain harbors and shipyards as bases for the repair of belligerent vessels and thus turn them into areas of war activity. Third, he will, if he deems it appropriate, assure the transfer of American goods to Great Britain by convoying them across the sea, because it certainly would defeat the intention of this act if the United States built ships by the hundreds and manufactured munitions in billion dollar lots on its own motion and then allowed German submarines and bombing planes to sink them in the ocean as fast as the United States can produce them.

Unless this bill is to be regarded as a mere rhetorical flourish—and respect for its authors precludes the thought of such frivolity—then, I submit, it is a bill for waging an undeclared war. We should entertain no delusions on this point. We should now face frankly and with such knowledge and intelligence as we may have the nature and probable consequences of that war. Without indulging in recriminations, we are bound to consider that fateful prospect.

We, however, poised now on the brink of the fateful decision respecting ourselves, are under positive obligation to discuss the aims of the Government of the United States in the activities which would be let loose under this bill, if enacted. Indeed it becomes the solemn duty of all Members of Congress to do this. If they are not to vote thoughtlessly and recklessly, they will ask themselves certain grave questions before they vote. And I may say, gentlemen of the committee, I do not envy you that solemn task that falls upon you. Congress cannot in truth escape these questions, for it will be answering them if it passes this bill—answering them conceivably in a manner fraught with infinite tragedy for the United States.

Here are the questions:

Does Congress intend to guarantee the present extent, economic resources, and economic methods of the British Empire forever to the Government of Great Britain by placing the unlimited resources of the United States forever at the disposal of the British Government, however constituted?

Does Congress intend to supply money, ships, and commodities of war until the French Republic is restored? until the integrity of its empire is assured? until all the lands run over by Hitler are once more vested with full sovereignty? until Russia has returned to Finland and Poland the territories wrested from them? until democracy is reestablished in Greece? until the King of Albania has recovered his throne?

Is Congress prepared to pour out American wealth until the Chungking government in China has conquered the Nanking government? Until Japan is expelled from the continent? Until Chinese Communists are finally suppressed? And until Soviet Russia is pushed back within the old Russian borders?

And if European or Asiatic powers should propose to make settlements without providing democracy, a bill of rights, and economic security for everybody, everywhere, will Congress insist that they keep on fighting until the President of the United States is satisfied with the results? If none of the countries deemed under the terms of this bill to be defending the United States succeeds in defeating its enemy with the material aid rendered by the United States, will Congress throw millions of boys after the billions in dollars?

DOCUMENT NO. 17

SENATOR ROBERT A. TAFT
WARNS AGAINST CONVOYS[*]

To anti-interventionists, the convoy issue was a crucial one. Roosevelt himself had told reporters in January 1941 that when a nation convoyed ships through a hostile zone, there was "apt to be shooting" and "shooting comes awfully close to war." In this selection, Taft offered the additional argument that American convoys were not necessary to Britain's survival.

γ   γ   γ

It is said that there is no use in manufacturing munitions and giving them to England unless we are prepared to guarantee that they are safely delivered in England. I suspect that the real purpose of advocating convoys is to provide an effective means of getting us into the war, rather than any concern about the arrival of our munitions. For it has now been made clear that in the first 4 months of this year less than 4 per cent of the ships carrying munitions from this country to Great Britain were actually sunk. These are the figures of the United States Maritime Commission, confirmed by the experience of the American Red Cross. When we consider also that our most valuable aid to England today is the supplying of bombing planes, and that these planes are flown over under their own power, the actual percentage of destruction is even less than 4 per cent. Furthermore, there is no assurance that if we convoy we can prevent sinkings, although we may somewhat reduce them. Apparently a considerable percentage of our munitions is destroyed after their arrival in England by the bombing of ships, docks, and warehouses in the harbors. Our convoys cannot prevent that destruction.

If what the administration wants to do is to aid England, it can accomplish a great deal more by speeding up production and eliminating strikes and providing a sensible Government set-up in Washington to secure that result. The argument for convoys is not sound, anyway. There is no reason why, because we choose to aid the British by making

[*]From Robert A. Taft, radio address of May 17, 1941, in Appendix, *Congressional Record*, entered May 19, 1941, p. A2343.

available in this country, free of charge, unlimited quantities of munitions, we should also assume voluntarily the burden of delivering those munitions in England and thereby go to war in England's behalf. England has more than half the merchant shipping of the world, a larger navy than we have, and control of the seas as much as seas can be controlled under modern conditions of warfare.

Think what the argument for convoys really implies. If it is sound to say that there is no use supplying munitions without delivering them, then it is just as sound to say that there is no use delivering munitions if the British have not enough men to handle them. Once we have convoys, the argument follows inevitably that we must send our Army to handle the growing flood of American munitions. Nothing is said now by the British about any shortage of men, but after a year and a half of war they have only been able to get a mixed force of 500,000 men to Africa, where they certainly need a million men today. The cry for men will follow the cry for convoys.

DOCUMENT NO. 18

AMERICA FIRST COMMITTEE
ON GERMAN CONQUEST OF RUSSIA[*]

The interventionists claimed that once Hitler commanded the massive resources of the Soviet Union, he would be close to world domination. In this reading, the America First Committee strongly challenged such a position, claiming that German conquest of the Soviet Union could weaken, not strengthen, Hitler's Reich.

γ   γ   γ

Did You Know #6 [see Document No. 25] analyzes the economic position of Germany, assuming that Hitler had conquered all of Europe plus the countries of Asia and Africa which border the Mediterranean Sea. The conclusion was that Nazi Europe would be forced to import even more food and raw materials, and discover even larger export markets for her manufactures than were required by the old Germany. Therefore, an enlarged Germany—despite her new "living space"—would be in no position to dictate the terms on which she would trade. Since June 22, interventionists have been making a great to-do over the effect of a possible Russian collapse. They have been seeing a Germany, already fat from the conquest of Western Europe, emerging from the Russian war still more powerful, and ready to run the world's international trade on any terms that Adolf Hitler might care to devise—with nobody in position to talk back. Actually, when the facts are examined, this nightmarish concept is seen to have little foundation. The conquest of Russia would contribute little to Germany's bargaining power. For the present, at least, it would contribute little to Germany's available wealth. That is if trade and production figures mean what they say. Germany's economy still would be unbalanced as ever . . . and the German dream of self-sufficiency as remote as ever from realization.

[*]From Research Division, America First Committee, "Swastika over Eagle," August 1, 1941, in Justus D. Doenecke, ed., *In Danger Undaunted: The Anti-interventionist Movement of 1940–1941 as Revealed in the Papers of the America First Committee* (Stanford, Calif.: Hoover Institution Press, 1990), pp. 164–165.

Big Picture

The effect on world commerce of the unification of Nazi Europe into one economy which included the whole of the continent west of the Soviet Union and all the countries of Africa and Asia bordering on the Mediterranean has been studied by Cleona Lewis of the Brookings Institution in her recent book "Nazi Europe and World Trade." Basing her study on the two carefully selected years 1937 and 1929, Dr. Lewis makes clear that such a Europe would be a net importer of food and many essential raw materials such as oil, copper and lead without which a modern industrial state cannot exist. Because Europe still would have to buy these materials Dr. Lewis concludes that Hitler would be no more able to dictate the terms of world trade than he was before the war. Europe simply does not produce enough food, and nobody can dig minerals from the earth which are not there. If the undeveloped expanses of the Soviet Union were to become a part of Nazi Europe—or Nazi Eurasia—Dr. Lewis finds that Germany's position would hardly be improved at all. Remember that a Nazi Europe includes the African and Near Eastern countries which border the Mediterranean, then add Russia. From Dr. Lewis's tables . . . the following facts can be deduced: Russia's *total* exports to *all* countries of foodstuffs amounted to only 14 per cent of a Nazi Europe's *net* imports of foodstuffs in 1937, to only 11 per cent in 1929; Russia's *total* exports to *all* countries of raw materials amounted to only 8 per cent of a Nazi Europe's *net* imports in 1937, to only 9 per cent in 1929. ("Net" figures are used for a Nazi Europe to allow for trade between countries included here in the total Nazi economy—such as wheat shipped from Algiers to Europe, or copper shipped from Cyprus.) Obviously, then, a Nazi economy that included Russia and the Baltic countries once dominated by Russia would still have to buy food and raw materials in the world market—or die.

DOCUMENT NO. 19

JOHN HAYNES HOLMES
ON RUSSIAN VICTORY[*]

In claiming that a victorious Soviet Union was a serious threat to Western democracy, Holmes was voicing a major fear of the anti-interventionists. For Holmes the matter was all the more poignant, because Holmes had been a spirited defender of the Russian regime. He later said in a sermon, "We permitted ourselves to condone wrongs that we knew must be wrong. We consented to violations of principle that we knew to be fatal to the moral integrity of mankind." In this following article Holmes sees the Soviet government as an external threat as well.

γ γ γ

Russia is in the war. Naturally enough, most Americans are rooting for Russia to win. But before we become emotionally too involved it would be well to consider what it might mean to have Russia win this war, or her particular share thereof. What would she get out of the struggle after it is all over? We may be sure that Russia is not going to fight through to victory for nothing. After she has scorched the earth of uncounted miles of her territory, laid down the lives of millions of her sons, seen her industries ruined, her cities bombed, her treasure wasted, and her dream of a Communist utopia postponed for a hundred years, if not altogether ruined, she is going to demand compensation in the settlement. Are we sure we are prepared to grant her demands?

Let us turn away from the battle for a moment and look into the future. Visualize the time when the fighting will be done and the peace must be made. What is Russia going to say and do?

. . . .

1. Russia will annex Finland. In 1940, Stalin will explain, Russia was very lenient with Finland. When Helsinki sued for peace after losing the inexcusable war of 1939–40, Moscow respected Finland's inde-

---

[*]From John Haynes Holmes, "If Russia Wins," *Christian Century* 58 (July 30, 1941): 954, 955. copyright 1941 Christian Century Foundation. Reprinted by permission from the December 11, 1940 issue of *The Christian Century*.

pendence and took only certain strategic points necessary to Russia's military security. Then, when Hitler pounced without warning upon the Soviets, Finland followed suit, and Marshal Mannerheim led Finnish armies onto Russian soil. There must now be left no danger of any repetition of this offense, Stalin will affirm. Leningrad must be made safe.

2. Russia will annex Latvia, Lithuania, and Estonia. Like Finland, these countries Stalin will explain, were a part of ancient Russia. The peasants and workers of these countries are entitled to enjoy the same proletarian emancipation that has been granted to the rest of the Russian people. Furthermore, these countries, like Finland, are necessary to Russia's military security. They are her bastions and bulwarks against the chaos of western Europe. So what was done at Versailles in 1919, and undone in 1940, must now be undone again, Stalin will say.

3. Russia will annex Poland, or at least that part of Poland which belonged to Russia before the way of 1914. It is true that the restoration of Poland was one of the noble fruits of the first World War. It is true that the new restoration of Poland, after the debacle of 1939 and the fourth partition of 1940, was one of the few perfectly distinct purposes of the second World War. What did Britain go to war for if not to save Poland? In what hope did Paderewski and all his heroic countrymen live in these last months, and Paderewski himself die, if not in the hope that Poland should be born anew? But Stalin will carefully explain that he shared in none of these promises. So far as the world knows, he gave no pledge to honor them when he joined the alliance with Britain. He has no sentiment about such things.

4. Russia will insist, under one form or another, on dominating the Balkans. Czechoslovakia, Hungary, Rumania, Bulgaria, Yugoslavia, Greece will fall under her sway as they now lie under Germany's sway. What more natural fruit of a victory in arms over Germany? And to these, undoubtedly, will be added the Dardanelles, as the key that turns the lock on all of eastern Europe.

5. Russia will probably demand East Prussia as her share of a dismembered Germany. Will Germany be dismembered? She certainly will, if this war is won by Britain and her allies. And in this division of the spoil, Russia will demand her ample portion.

6. After Europe, Asia. Here speculation is not so easy. But that Russia will openly and permanently take over Mongolia is probable; and that

she will seize Manchukuo from Japan is not improbable. Russia's hunger for Manchuria is as insatiable as her hunger for the Dardanelles. And then there will be the settlement for all the aid she has given to China and the payment of Stalin's debt to the Communist armies in that divided country.

DOCUMENT NO. 20

AMERICA FIRST COMMITTEE
ON INVASION DANGER*

This AFC memo was issued in response to Roosevelt's plea to retain draftees and national guardsmen in the army after their twelve month's term of service had expired. FDR also called upon Congress to declare a national emergency. Speaking on July 21, 1941, the president said, "I do believe—I know—the danger today is infinitely greater" than in the previous year. To the AFC Roosevelt had not yet justified any such emergency.

γ   γ   γ

Is there danger of invasion from the frozen tundra of eastern Siberia, across the barren wastes of Alaska into western Canada and our own Pacific Northwest?

But is Alaska a highway of invasion—whoever holds eastern Siberia? Independent experts say "No." Actually the alarmists who talk of invasion via Alaska are talking military nonsense. They ignore 1) the strategic difficulty of supplying and reinforcing the Siberian bases which can be reached only by boat and plane whoever holds them, 2) the growing formidability of our own network of naval and air bases in Alaska. Their fears have been best answered by Hanson W. Baldwin, military analyst for the *New York Times*, in his recent book, "United We Stand": "There has been much talk of 'the vulnerability of Alaska to invasion'. . . . But we could wish for no more ludicrous and fatal error on the part of an enemy than a landing in Alaska. . . . And if an enemy ever attempted an overland campaign striking for Seattle he would leave behind him a trail bleached in bones, and in the words of one officer, the soldiers who started would not reach Seattle. Their grandchildren might, but they would not be an army. . . . In the hysteria of the moment every area has suddenly become 'vital' and 'vulnerable'; even Alaska, wilderness of pine and snow, total population 73,000 people

*From Research Division, America First Committee, "Nobody Know the Trouble We're In," July 24, 1941, in Justus D. Doenecke, ed., *In Danger Undaunted: The Anti-interventionist Movement of 1940–1941 as Revealed in the Papers of the America First Committee* (Stanford, Calif.: Hoover Institution Press, 1990), pp. 362–365.

without a good air target in the territory, has been represented by sources that should know better as highly vulnerable to air attack."

Is there danger of invasion via Iceland, Greenland, Newfoundland and eastern Canada?

However, if ever there was a threat of invasion via Iceland, Greenland and Newfoundland, that threat has now been blocked. In August 1940, the President concluded a joint defense agreement with Canada. In September 1940, the President secured base rights in Newfoundland from Britain. In April 1941, the President made an executive agreement with the Danish Minister to Washington by which the U.S. secured base rights in Greenland. As if that were not enough, the President has now sent U.S. sailors and marines to Iceland. (On none of these agreements was Congress consulted.)

Is there danger of invasion via the Caribbean, which would drive a wedge between North and South America and threaten the Panama Canal?

If ever there was a serious threat via the Caribbean, it ceased to exist when the new Caribbean bases were acquired from Britain in September 1940. (Whether it was necessary to give away fifty destroyers to acquire them is another question.) The Caribbean now is literally ringed with bases—Guantanamo, Jamaica, Puerto Rico, Virgin Islands, Antigua, Saint Lucia, Trinidad. The southern approach is sealed by bases in British Guiana, the northern approach by a base in the Bahamas, and Vichy-owned Martinique is virtually surrounded. Secretary of the Navy Frank Knox has testified that the Caribbean is now "substantially an American lake."

Is there danger of invasion of Brazil from Dakar in West Africa or from the islands of the Atlantic?

A squalid, tropical port, Dakar is not suitable now as an invasion base, and it would take several years to make it suitable. Moreover, there are many indications that lead to the belief that Brazil may be about to enter into a cooperative defense agreement with the U.S. which would include base rights on the Brazilian bulge. Should this happen, the last argument for seizing Dakar—as a defense measure—would disappear.

And bases in Brazil would minimize whatever real danger there is of a Fifth Column uprising in Brazil. . . . What is true of Dakar is true of the Atlantic islands—the Cape Verdes, the Canaries, the Azores, Madeira. Moreover, to take Dakar or the islands would require 100,000 men, a huge fleet of perhaps 100 transports, and a large naval escort.

DOCUMENT NO. 21

AMERICA FIRST COMMITTEE
ON ATLANTIC CHARTER[*]

Here the AFC found the Atlantic Charter unenforceable. It begins its comments with a quotation from Winston Churchill, who, in The Aftermath *(1929), had commented on the vagueness of Woodrow Wilson's peace aims as espoused in the president's address to Congress of January 8, 1918: "These 'Fourteen Points,' admirably, if vaguely, phrased considered in the main of broad principles which could be applied in varying degrees according to the fortunes of war. . . . None of them [the Allies] was concerned to examine the whole speech meticulously or felt compelled except in general sympathy." As this reading shows, the AFC not only found the Atlantic Charter vague but ineffectual.*

γ   γ   γ

Second, they desire to see no territorial changes that do not accord with the freely expressed wishes of the people concerned.

Again granting the sincerity of the two men, difficulties loom up when the practical working-out of this idealistic sentiment is considered. . . . it may be asked whether or not, at the war's end, it will be *militarily expedient* for Britain and the United States to withdraw their troops from Iceland. Will their new ally, Russia, seek to regain the eastern half of Poland which the Communists took over at the same time the Germans seized the western portion? And if so, to what extent, if any, are the United States and the United Kingdom committed to preventing such action? Will Britain give up Iraq, or will she feel that because of unsettled post-war conditions, and the appetite of the Russian bear, Empire troops must remain stationed there? And for how long? Will Greece feel that because of her sacrifices she is entitled to wrest control of the nearby Dodecanese Islands from Italy? What about the territory now controlled by the Free French forces of General Charles DeGaulle? . . .

[*]From Research Division, America First Committee, "Eight Points for War or Peace: 3) Can They Work?" September 2, 1941, in Justus D. Doenecke, ed., *In Danger Undaunted: The Anti-interventionist Movement of 1940–1941 as Revealed in the Papers of the America First Committee* (Stanford, Calif.: Hoover Institution Press, 1990), pp. 333–336.

Third, they respect the right of all peoples to choose the form of government under which they will live; and they wish to see sovereign rights and self government restored to those who have been forcibly deprived of them.

Naturally, with Communist Dictator Stalin as their ally, neither Churchill nor Roosevelt could presume to lay down the type of government which they will permit in the world after the war is over. To have insisted that all governments become democracies would not only have alienated their new ally, but might also have disturbed some of the present heads of Latin American governments whose goodwill is now so essential to the plan of Western Hemisphere defense. The result at the end of the war may be that Russia will dominate Eastern Europe and much of Asia. What that means to the rights of those countries adjacent to Russia can be deduced from the fate which befell Poland and the small Baltic nations into which Russia marched after the 1939 Nazi-Soviet pact.

What considerations will determine the new boundary lines—economic? military? political? historical? geographic? language? balance of power? If historical precedents are to be considered, what is to be done in the case of Poland, for instance, whose boundary lines have shifted at frequent intervals through the centuries? Which boundary line in what century shall be considered the correct one?

Point Three also "wishes" to see "sovereign rights" restored to those who have been forcibly deprived of them. It is quite apparent that this wish is directed at restoring the present Allied Governments-in-exile to their former ruling positions. Whether or not such a step would be a move forward for democracy is a question worth pondering. Some of the royal rulers now living in London awaiting their return to thrones are: King Zog of Albania, King Haakon VII of Norway, King Peter of Yugoslavia, and King George of Greece (who after the 1923 revolution in Greece lived in London until restored to the throne in 1935). Unlike the other royal refugees, Queen Wilhelmina of the Netherlands still rules over an empire, although the Netherlands itself is German-occupied territory. Of Wilhelmina's 67,290,000 subjects, only 8,800,000 live in the mother country itself. The rest live across the oceans in the colonial possessions—the Dutch East Indies in the Pacific; the Dutch West Indies in the Caribbean; and Dutch Guiana in South America— all of which continue to take orders from their Queen. (*Washington Post*, August 10, 1941.)

DOCUMENT NO. 22

UNCENSORED ON ATLANTIC CHARTER[*]

Unlike the Chicago Tribune *and many conservative backers of the America First Committee, the weekly mimeographed newsletter* Uncensored *was unabashedly liberal in its views. At the time that it published the following critique, it was edited by Sidney Hertzberg, a prominent Socialist journalist, and Cushman Reynolds, coauthor of* Strategy of the Americas (1941). *In this selection one finds close attention to the language of the Charter.*

γ γ γ

PLATFORM

The Joint Declaration by Roosevelt and Churchill is neither a Magna Carta nor a Declaration of Independence. It has not and apparently is not going to fire the imagination of men who would be free. As social documents go, the eight points fall into the category in which the platforms of the Democratic and Republican parties belong. Its joints are exposed. It was constructed to please the most and offend the fewest among the conglomeration of forces threatened by the Axis. It should be analyzed on this basis.

"First: Their countries seek no aggrandizement, territorial or other." Neither the U.S. nor Britain have any economic need for territorial expansion. Since the war began, large chunks of Africa have come under British control. Presumably their future will be settled in accordance with other points in the declaration.

"Second: They desire to see no territorial changes that do not accord with the freely expressed wishes of the peoples concerned." The "desire" may not necessarily coincide with the actuality. Nations that have enough and are fighting for the status quo ante bellum obviously have no interest in territorial changes.

"Third: They respect the right of all peoples to choose the form of government under which they will live; and they wish to see sovereign rights and self-government restored to those who have been

[*]"Platform," *Uncensored*, No. 98, August 16, 1941, pp. 1–2.

forcibly deprived of them." Restoration of the Versailles Ruritanias
is a prospect that would be relished only by the exiled Ruritanians
who are useful to Britain just now. No definite promise is involved.
Roosevelt and Churchill "wish to see" it happen. Eight of Wilson's
14 points were definite commitments—naming names—for the
restoration of national sovereignties. "Respect" for the right of
peoples to choose their own form of government may amount to
nothing more than Britain's "respect" for that right in India has
in the past.

"Fourth: They will endeavor, with due respect for their existing obligations, to further the enjoyment by all States, great or small, victor
or vanquished, of access, on equal terms, to the trade and to the
raw materials of the world which are needed for their economic
prosperity." For imperialists the saving phrase here is, "with due
respect for their existing obligations." These obligations now include: the British Empire; the Ottawa Agreement; the tariff and
gold policies of the U.S.; the international cartels which gave Britain world control of such products as rubber and tin. They may
even include the blocked sterling "agreements" which Britain has
made with the new territory she controls in Africa.

"Fifth: They desire to bring about the fullest collaboration between all
nations in the economic field with the object of securing, for all,
improved labor standards, economic adjustment and social security." This point belongs to British Labor and U.S. New Dealers.
The idea has had a workout in the International Labor Office
which found its achievements limited by the labor practices of its
member nations.

"Sixth: After the final destruction of the Nazi tyranny, they hope to see
established a peace which will afford to all nations the means of
dwelling in safety within their own boundaries, and which will afford assurance that all the men in all the lands may live out their
lives in freedom from fear and want." It may be of definite significance that the destruction of Nazi "tyranny" rather than of the
Nazi regime is specified. Two of the four freedoms are strangely
absent: freedom of speech and freedom of worship. The omission
of either or both may be a sop to Stalin.

"Seventh: Such a peace should enable all men to traverse the high seas and oceans without hindrance." Obviously the two greatest maritime powers will insist on that hoary hoax, "freedom of the seas." In peacetime, the seas are free for everyone—for the British as well as the Nicaraguan merchant marine. In war, there never has been or will be freedom of the seas; there is only the British and/or the U.S. fleets.

Eighth: (disarmament of aggressors is "essential"). Disarmament of Germany after the war is less extreme than dismemberment, but it will probably satisfy the racists who maintain that Germans are congenital brutes. Disarmament of Germany would mean an Allied army of occupation. It would again make Germany a pariah among nations and an easy prey for Hitler-like demagogues.

DOCUMENT NO. 23

AMERICA FIRST COMMITTEE
ON FREEDOM OF THE SEAS*

Here the AFC accuses Roosevelt of surreptitiously engaging in convoy protection of Allied ships, a violation—it claimed—of the cash-and-carry law passed in the fall of 1939. In effect, the AFC claimed that the president had initiated an undeclared war without popular consent.

γ   γ   γ

Danger Through Subterfuge

The President has sought to use the national policy of aid short of war to Britain in order to circumvent the Neutrality Act. The "bridge of ships" across the Atlantic of which he frequently speaks, the occupation of Iceland chiefly for the purpose of enabling shipment of war supplies there in American ships, thence to be transshipped to British or other Allied ships. . . . are steps which necessarily place American ships and citizens in danger zones. The naval and air patrols of the Atlantic waters which the President established in April, 1941 (*New York Times*, April 29, 1941) were designed less for actual American defense purposes than for the purpose of aiding British convoy shipments. Such patrols, because they give actual assistance and advice to British warships, have been denounced by one constitutional authority as unconstitutional "acts of war" (Henry Frazer, *Syracuse Post Standard*, May 11, 1941). They necessarily place American warships and American sailors and aviators in shooting zones. The widespread transfer of American ships to the flag of Panama, even State Department officials now admit, was done in order to circumvent the Neutrality Act and to allow those ships to travel in war zones (*Washington Times-Herald*, Sept. 13, 1941).

Research Division, America First Committee, "One-Man War," September 13, 1941, in Justus D. Doenecke, ed., *In Danger Undaunted: The Anti-interventionist Movement of 1940–1941 as Revealed in the Papers of the America First Committee* (Stanford, Calif.: Hoover Institution Press, 1990), pp. 405–406.

Convoys

Nor can the President's "shoot on sight" order be justified, as he claims, as necessary to protect "freedom of the seas." It must be recalled that American armed protection is to be given, not only to American ships, but also to the ships of any flag, and that the waters in which the protection is to be given extend to an undefined width (even to the Pacific Ocean), to any waters the President chooses to declare vital to our "defense." This would enable our fleet to give what amounts to "convoy protection" to British ships or the ships of any other allied nation, as well as American ships, carrying war supplies for Britain or Russia or China. It would enable American patrols even to convoy British ships right into English ports, since the President has stated that he did not feel that the Neutrality Law prevented American warships from entering the war zones he established under that law (*New York Times*, April 29, 1941).

Freedom of the Seas

What the President calls "freedom of the seas" is a misnomer. It is neither the "traditional American doctrine," nor any doctrine recognized in international law. What he asked in reality was the "freedom to aid at will one belligerent nation without danger of interference by the other belligerent"—a freedom which our own government and the British government have denied on past occasions, and which the British would be the first to reject now, if it were to their advantage.

. . . .

Congress "Eliminated"

The most serious ultimate consequence of the President's "shoot on sight" order is its effect on our form of representative government. His order does not eliminate submarines; as one newspaper editorial points out, it eliminates Congress (*Washington Times-Herald*, Sept. 13, 1941). The President unquestionably acted without consultation with Congress because of his knowledge that the overwhelming majority of Congress, like the American people, are opposed to participation in a "shooting war." His action seeks to arrogate unto himself the warmaking power entrusted by our Constitution to Congress alone. His powers as Commander-in-Chief of the Army and Navy clearly cannot be used to destroy another constitutional provision, the war-making power of Congress, since, as the Supreme Court has pointed out, even his powers in the field of international relations must be exercised in compliance with the mandates of the Constitution (U.S. v. Curtiss-Wright Export Corp.; 299 U.S., 304, 319–22).

DOCUMENT NO. 24

AMERICA FIRST COMMITTEE
ON PANAMANIAN REGISTRY[*]

The following AFC memo was triggered by the sinking of the U.S. freighter Pink Star *on September 19, 1941. The ship was sailing under the Panamanian flag to avoid the restrictions of the Cash–and–Carry Act of 1939 and the Lend–Lease bill.*

γ   γ   γ

Ships in War Trade

The Nazi technique of submarine warfare is unquestionably ruthless. But examination of the facts involved in these sinkings demonstrates that the Administration is scarcely in a position to claim that the ships which were sunk were legally immune from attack and entitled to the protection of the American flag. The *Pink Star* was a Danish ship which had been seized by the United States under the recent law for the seizure of foreign ships in American ports. It was chartered by the Maritime Commission to the United States Lines, a private concern, and registered under the flag of Panama. It was therefore not an American-flag ship and was not entitled to the protection of the United States. No American citizens were on the ship, when she was sunk between Iceland and Greenland, *on her way to Britain* (Washington Times Herald, Sept. 23, 1941). The *Sessa* and the *Montana* were also Danish ships which had been seized similarly, chartered to a private American firm, and also registered under the flag of Panama. Both were sunk near Iceland while carrying cargoes to Iceland (*New York Times*, Sept. 10, 13, 1941). Only one American was on board the *Sessa*, and none on the *Montana*. As has been pointed out . . . , the *Steel Seafarer*, sailing under the American flag, was sunk in the Red Sea, 12,000 miles from the U.S., while carrying contraband war supplies for Britain. The ship was legally present in that area only because President Roosevelt had revoked his proclamation

[*]From Research Division, America First Committee, "Jekyll-and-Hyde Ships," September 23, 1941, in Justus D. Doenecke, ed., *In Danger Undaunted: The Anti-interventionist Movement of 1940–1941 as Revealed in the Papers of the America First Committee* (Stanford, Calif.: Hoover Institution Press, 1990), pp. 411–413.

declaring the Red Sea a war zone and forbidding American ships to travel there—a proclamation made in compliance with the mandate of the Neutrality Act. The *Robin Moor*, also under the American flag, was carrying contraband to another country at war (British South Africa), and was sunk in the South Atlantic. . . . In neither, case were any American lives lost.

Seafaring Panama

The cases of the *Pink Star*, the *Sessa* and the *Montana* are of the most interest because they illustrate strikingly the type of subterfuge used by the Administration to evade the clear intent of the Neutrality Act and the Lease-Lend law. These three ships and sixty other American-owned ships suitable for transatlantic trade have been transferred to the flag of Panama between the outbreak of the European war (Sept. 1, 1939) and July 1, 1941. The 63 transferred ships comprise a tonnage of 358,460 tons—a tonnage large enough to rank little Panama as one of the leading shipping nations in the world (Bulletin of American Bureau of Shipping, Sept., 1941; figures supplied by U.S. Maritime Commission). The absurdity of the situation is evident when it is recalled that Panama's area (33,667 sq. miles) is less than that of the state of Indiana, which itself ranks 37th among the states of the Union in area, and that the population of Panama is less than that of the District of Columbia (World Almanac, 1940). Among the 63 transferred ships are 28 tankers (Bulletin of the American Bureau of Shipping, Sept., 1941). Yet the Administration recently claimed (until that claim was exploded by Congressional inquiry—see . . .) that there was an oil shortage on the East Coast because of the lack of tankers.

. . . .

Ships of Dual Personality

But even that policy could not justify sending supplies directly to countries at war, in American-flag ships. Consequently, the device was adopted of transferring American ships to the flag of Panama. It is now openly admitted that these transfers were made in order to evade the restrictions of the Neutrality Act (*Washington Times-Herald*, Sept. 13, 1941; *New York Times*, Sept. 23, 1941). Thus, on the one hand, the Administration seeks to place American ships in the war trade forbidden by our laws, by placing them under foreign flags, and, on the other hand, claims that *American* ships are being attacked when those foreign-flag ships run the risks to which that policy necessarily subjects them. The *Pink Star*, carrying a cargo to Britain, illustrates the dilemma perfectly. But even the Administration must be reminded that it can't eat its cake and have it, too. Nor can it be claimed that we must protect these ships under the Panama flag on the theory that such protection is essential to hemisphere defense. These ships, carrying cargoes to countries at war in Europe, are not engaged in any activity essential to the defense of the Western Hemisphere.

DOCUMENT NO. 25

AMERICA FIRST COMMITTEE
ON NAZI TRADE THREAT[*]

On May 27, 1941, Roosevelt delivered a radio address in which he proclaimed an unlimited national emergency. In this "fireside chat," he claimed that a victorious Axis "would foster an economic stranglehold upon our several nations." Indeed Hitler would not only establish wages and hours but set the very profits American farmers would receive for their produce. This AFC memo takes issue with the president, declaring that even if the Germans dominated Europe and the Mediterranean, they could not control U.S. commerce.

γ   γ   γ

We can test the "economic" theory. Assume that the Nazis have military control of the entire continent of Europe (for the moment we can except the Soviet Union and the Soviet-dominated states). Make the further (and unlikely) assumption that they are able to unify the numerous nationalities of Europe, suppress or alleviate the age-old hatreds, obtain willing and eager cooperation from the sullen millions of their victims, and co-ordinate the productive capacities of the continent into one integrated, centrally controlled, economic and political unit. That unit would comprise twenty-one countries (Albania, Austria, Belgium, Luxembourg, Bulgaria, Czechoslovakia, Denmark, France, Germany, Greece, Hungary, Italy, Netherlands, Norway, Poland, Portugal, Rumania, Spain, Sweden, Switzerland, and Yugoslavia). Assume further that the Nazis are able to bring into that unit the eleven non-European countries which border the Mediterranean Sea (Algeria, Morocco, Tunisia, Libya, Tangier Zone, Egypt, Turkey, Syria, Lebanon, Palestine and Cyprus). Such assumptions are more than generous to the advocates of the "economic" theory of conquest: they give the Nazis control over countries in Europe, North Africa and the Near East which are yet unconquered.

[*]From Research Division, America First Committee, "Buy or Die," July 5, 1941, in Justus D. Doenecke, ed., *In Danger Undaunted: The Anti-interventionist Movement of 1940–1941 as Revealed in the Papers of the America First Committee* (Stanford, Calif.: Hoover Institution Press, 1990), pp. 159, 160, 161–162.

The popular impression fostered by interventionists is based on the assumption that the Nazi regime has been greatly strengthened economically by its conquests, especially in its power to influence trade relations with the nations of the Western Hemisphere. That impression is shown to be far from accurate in a current study published by the Brookings Institution, a conservative and eminently authoritative research institution ("Nazi Europe and World Trade," by Cleona Lewis, published in June, 1941). In this memorandum are discussed the resources and needs of a Nazi-controlled Europe as Dr. Lewis has analysed them. . . .

The study shows clearly that Nazi Europe—if it ever comes—will be in no position to dictate the nature and terms of world trade or of the trade of the Western Hemisphere countries. Paradoxical as it may sound, "Germany's supply problem has not been solved by her seizure of neighboring territories. On the contrary, it has been made more difficult. Raw-material imports, in particular, are considerably larger for the whole area than they were for Germany alone—whether they are measured in absolute or relative terms". . . . Despite the fact that Nazi Europe furnishes the "living space" the Nazis claimed was vital to Germany's existence, Germany's trade position is now weaker than before the war.

This is because Germany, before entry upon her career of aggression, was ultimately dependent upon outside sources for food and raw materials. Far from attaining independence of foreign sources for food and raw materials by her conquests, Germany has become more dependent than ever before upon foreign sources. The old Reich, both in 1929 and 1937, managed to maintain a slightly larger volume of exports than of imports, to sell more than she bought. Consequently she was in a position to drive a good bargain (page 178). Her foreign trade was fairly stable from 1925 through 1937, with foods and raw materials accounting for about 90%, usually, of her imports, and manufactured goods making up from 65% to 80% of her exports. This ratio held good, in the main, even despite the much-exaggerated Nazi trade drive and Nazi attempts to force surplus manufactured goods down the throats of Latin American and other foreign trade countries. . . .

Of the 20 European countries assumed to be under Nazi sway, only three really complement and help the Nazi economy by being exporters of foods and raw materials, and importers of manufactures (Bulgaria, Rumania, Yugoslavia). Ten others are helpful to the Nazis in part. Six of these (Denmark, Hungary, Netherlands, Poland, Portugal, and Spain) dovetail with the German economy in that they export more food than they buy, and import more manufactured goods than they sell; but they are dependent, like the old Germany, for most of their raw materials on outside sources. The four others in this second group (Albania, Greece, Norway, and Sweden) also help the old Reich in that they can supply raw materials and buy manufactures; but these countries are a detriment in that they must buy foods from outside sources. The last six [seven] states (Austria, Belgium, Luxembourg, Czechoslovakia, France, Italy, Switzerland) are like Germany in that they must sell their manufactured goods to the outside world, and must buy foods and raw materials. These are the large industrial countries whose subjugation is popularly supposed to constitute a great triumph for the Nazis. Actually, they furnish little opportunity for additional economic "living space." Once they are linked with Germany as a unit in Nazi Europe, they must buy from outside sources twice as much foodstuffs as the old Reich and almost three times as many raw materials, and they must sell almost twice as many manufactures. They have made Germany's presumed goal, independence of outside sources, much more difficult of attainment. . . .

These figures are not changed materially even if the Nazis control the eleven non-European countries bordering the Mediterranean Sea. On the basis of 1937 data, the latter provide only about 19% of the food and 8% of the raw materials needed by Nazi Europe, and take only 16% of the manufactured goods which Nazi Europe must sell. In short, "larger Germany would have to import more food and raw materials, and find larger markets for manufactures, than were required for the old Reich". . . .

The subjugation of Russia would not ease the economic problems of a Nazi Europe as much as has been popularly supposed. In 1929 and 1937 Russia's exports of foods and raw materials amounted to no more than four percent of Nazi Europe's needs (including Mediterranean countries). Nor is Russia much of a market for Nazi Europe's manufactured goods. . . .

Nazi Europe therefore must import or die. Without food imports, Europe's population must go on short rations, because of shortages of cereals, fats, vegetable oils, meats, and dairy products. Without raw material imports, the textile industries would be crippled (for lack of sufficient supplies of cotton, wool, silk, jute, flax and hemp); the leatherworking industries would be gravely impaired; large-scale synthetic rubber production would be necessary, which would in turn create new raw material needs. Without industrial mineral imports, "manufacturing, mining, transportation, communication and even agriculture would be severely handicapped." Machines and machine tools could no longer be made because of the lack of alloy metals and bearing metals. The automotive and electrical industries would suffer from lack of asbestos, mica, non-synthetic oils, copper and other minerals. There would be enough coal unless (a very likely probability) the resort to synthetic production of rubber, hosiery, and gasoline caused a coal shortage. . . .

Nazi Europe will have to import. Without imports, even the manufacture of the goods which she must sell in order to buy more foods and more raw materials will be crippled. Nazi Europe will be in no position to buy or not to buy, as she pleases, and therefore drive a hard bargain or dictate her own terms. *The bargaining advantage will rest with the Western Hemisphere countries and the other countries of the world which have for sale the products Nazi Europe needs.*

DOCUMENT NO. 26

GEORGE N. PEEK ON AXIS
IMPOVERISHING AMERICA*

Peek, a former president of the Moline Plow Company, had briefly directed a major New Deal agency, the Agricultural Adjustment Administration. Then, from 1933 to 1945, he was Roosevelt's special adviser on foreign trade. He resigned, however, in protest against reciprocal trade, a policy he deemed "unilateral economic disarmament," and became a strong critic of all New Deal policies. In this reading he outlines a strategy for economic survival.

γ   γ   γ

Competition is the life of trade and is always a threat in private business, no matter from whom it comes. So it is with nations.

Political control is one thing—economic necessity quite another. Now, let us get this straight. There is no difference in principle between foreign and domestic trade, except as restrictions have been imposed upon the entry of goods and the transfer of funds between countries. The war interventionists' theory is that one party to a transaction could dictate all the terms and conditions of the trade between two or more parties. How false. Every man, woman, and child knows better if he will think but for a moment. It takes two parties to complete a trade. The necessities and the desires of each are basic. To assume that one may dictate all the terms and conditions is assuming something which is not so. Therefore their case rests on a false premise and should be dismissed. As to Hitler's ability to dictate terms of trade to us in the event of a victory—no; that is where economic necessity comes into play. . . .

But under German control of Europe and other areas won't the conditions be so different that former rules will not apply?

Answer. First and foremost in importance is our great market. We have the greatest consuming power in the world. Our purchases from foreign countries support a large part of the economy of many of them. For example:

*From George N. Peek, memorandum to America First Committee, May 14, 1941, in Appendix, *Congressional Record*, entered May 19, 1941, pp. A2368–2369.

Latin America produces 90 percent of all the coffee—we consume half of it. Europe, too, depends upon Latin America for her supply—about the same quantity as ours—although she has four times our population.

The Malay States, the Dutch East Indies, and small neighboring countries produce nearly 95 percent of the rubber and, including China, 60 percent of the tin. We use half of the rubber and 40 percent of the world's production of tin.

Japan produces nearly 90 percent of the silk; we buy 90 percent of her exports.

These are examples of the dependency of foreign nations upon our market. Others may be cited—that is, jute from India, diamonds and gold from South Africa, tea from southeastern Asia, etc.

The economy of such nations does not shift with the flag of the overlord. It relies upon our markets. It does not change with super-political control. . . .

Then comes the question of technological development and the use of substitutes. Great progress has been made in this field in recent years.

The development of synthetic rubber has progressed to a point where we may say that, if necessary, we are no longer dependent upon the Eastern Hemisphere. Within a very few years we could produce our own rubber, as Germany has done. A number of our most important concerns are active in this field.

The same thing may be said of silk. Witness the great development of rayon and now nylon.

We are now preparing to smelt a considerable portion of our tin requirements in the United States from ore coming from Latin America. In addition, important substitutes have been developed from plastics and other materials, replacing tin.

This hemisphere can supply our manganese and potash—the former through the development of machinery and processes of refining low-grade ores here and in Cuba, and the latter through the development of our own mines.

These are examples only. There is great progress in other fields. . . .

Question 3. If Germany, producing with slave labor, can offer better prices to Latin America, how can we compete?

Answer. That is a trick question. The term "Latin America" covers many countries and a wide diversity of economic interests. It must be remembered that Germany, and England, too, had substantial trade with South America before World War No. 1. There is nothing new about competition with them, except in degree. There are many considerations involved in trade besides price. Design and adaptability of products to do the work desired; terms, delivery dates; personal equation between buyer and seller; and numerous other things. Frequently we hear the phrase, "Quality is remembered long after price is forgotten." If price were the sole measuring stick, the manufacturer with the lowest price would be selling all the goods, be they automobiles or what. Competition would die. Monopoly would succeed it, and higher prices might then result.

The answer lies in mutuality of interest between nations and regional economic areas, all things considered. Under these circumstances there is only one intelligent procedure for us to follow, and that is to recognize the conditions under which trade is now conducted between nations, and then, so long as governments control the foreign trade of their nationals, negotiate country by country for the terms and conditions under which goods may be exchanged satisfactorily. Each country must recognize frankly the needs of the other.

Other things being equal, free labor can out-produce slave labor. We made our greatest progress after we abolished slavery—slave labor produces little buying power. American wage levels support our higher American standards of living. They protect the American workers on our farms and in our factories against the lower standards not only of the forced labor of the Axis Powers and Russia but of the low-paid labor of the Argentine and China and the cheaper labor everywhere outside the United States of America. Our wage levels must be insulated against the competition of a world turned upside down.

DOCUMENT NO. 27

ANNE MORROW LINDBERGH
AND THE WAVE OF THE FUTURE*

Anne Morrow Lindbergh, the wife of Charles A. Lindbergh, is a prominent poet and writer. In her forty-one page book The Wave of the Future *(1940), she stressed that the United States should not face the new world of dictatorships by entering into a destructive war. Rather it must continue to foster domestic reform. Contrary to myth, she did not claim that the specific "wave" was totalitarianism; instead it represented a new scientific, mechanized, and material era of civilization. Seeing how the very phrase "wave of the future" was misinterpreted as an apology for fascism, she wrote in her diary, "Will I have to bear this lie throughout life?" In the following selection, she denies that "the things we dislike in Nazism" are the forces of the future."*

γ   γ   γ

No, I cannot see the war as a "crusade." If I could label it at all, I would label it part of a vast revolution. I am not here defending the forms this revolution has taken: aggression, terror, class or race persecution. I oppose these as deeply as any American. But I do feel that had the world been able, by peaceful revolution, to foresee and forestall the changes, to correct the abuses that pushed behind the Communist and Fascist revolutions, we would not now have to come to them by such terrible means. The world has been forced to its knees. Unhappily, we seldom find our way there without being beaten to it by suffering.

I cannot see this war, then, simply and purely as a struggle between the "Forces of Good" and the "Forces of Evil." If I could simplify it into a phrase at all, it would seem truer to say that the "Forces of the Past" are fighting against the "Forces of the Future." The tragedy is, to the honest spectator, that there is so much that is good in the "Forces of the Past," and so much that is evil in the "Forces of the Future."

To make this statement is not to say that "might makes right," or that it is Germany's "turn to win," or to give any such literal and facile ex-

*Excerpt from *The Wave of the Future: A Confession of Faith*, copyright 1940 and renewed by Anne Morrow Lindbergh, reprinted by permission of Harcourt Brace & Company, pp. 17–19, 22–27.

planations. It is not to claim that the things we dislike in Naziism *are* the forces of the future. But it is to say that somehow the leaders in Germany, Italy and Russia have discovered how to use new social and economic forces; very often they have used them badly, but nevertheless, they have recognized and used them. They have sensed the changes and they have exploited them. They have felt the wave of the future and they have leapt upon it. The evils we deplore in these systems are not in themselves the future; they are scum on the wave of the future. . . .

What I question is the confident assumption that this way of life—in which I include our own here in the United States—will still be there after the war is over, even if Great Britain wins; or that it would have continued for long, unchanged, had there been no war. A world in which there were widespread depressions, millions of unemployed, and drifting populations was not going to continue indefinitely. A world in which young people, willing to work, could not afford a home and family, in which the race declined in hardiness, in which one found on every side dissatisfaction, maladjustment and moral decay—that world was ripe for change. That it had to die in violence is the catastrophe; that it had to die in misery, terror and chaos; that it had to fall, dragging down with it much that was good and beautiful and right, spilling the blood, wasting the lives, warping the spirit of many who were needed for the reconstruction of the new world; that it had to die in war, which carries in its train those very miseries it seeks to escape.

I always hoped war could be avoided, or that an early peace would still save some part of a world I loved—that the good of a dying civilization could be bequeathed in comparative tranquility to the new one; as, in nature, a flower dies, but the plant puts forth a new bud from the old stem. All chance for peaceful transition passes more irretrievably with each day that the war continues. The old world we loved is going, and I doubt very much that what immediately follows—if every nation blazes in the same conflagration—will be appreciably better, even in the "Democracies," than what we have witnessed in Germany lately. In other words, I do not believe the things we condemn in Germany are innately German; but rather that they are born of war, revolution, defeat, frustration and suffering. They are evils which may come to every nation under the same conditions—conditions that are increasing in likelihood for the majority of the world with each day this war is prolonged.

What, then, is your conclusion to this discussion? may be justly asked of me. Do you urge a defeatist acceptance of the inevitable? Do you want us to concur in the violent forms (you say you oppose) of the revolution that is now going on in Europe? Should we advocate the overthrow of fundamental principles underlying our way of life? Should we go against our hearts, our faiths, our beliefs—all we love—and encourage the things we hate, in order to follow a will-o'-the-wisp, fatalistic and planetary conception that "All is for the best in the best of possible worlds"?

No, I cannot pledge my personal allegiance to those systems I disapprove of, or those barbarisms I oppose from the bottom of my heart, even if they *are* on the wave of the future. Nor do I propose the surrender of our basic beliefs. But I do feel that it is futile to get into a hopeless "crusade" to "save" civilization. I do not believe civilization can be "saved" simply by going to war. Neither can "democracy" or "liberty" or "our way of life" be saved by any such negative point of view. If we do not *better* our civilization, our way of life, and our democracy, there will be no use trying to "save" them by fighting; they will crumble away under the very feet of our armies.

It seems to me that our task, instead of crusading against an inevitable "revolution," or change, in Europe, is to work toward a peaceful "revolution" here, or, rather, a reformation—to reform at home rather than crusade abroad. Our "revolution" will not take the form of a German, an Italian or a Russian revolution. Our answer to the world's problems is not their answer. It will not be the answer France is trying desperately to work out at this moment—and I have such faith in the French that I feel convinced that their ultimate contribution to the future will be even more beautiful than their contribution to the past. It will not be the answer that England will eventually find—though one cannot doubt that the great qualities of the English will be needed and will help to build the new world after this war is over.

Our answer should not and will not be the answer of any European nation. It should be a solution peculiarly and saltily our own. . . .

To desire a purely American solution is not to advocate strict "Isolationism." In national as in personal life, strict "Isolationism" seems to me a miserable ideal. But in both levels of living, most of us feel that our *first* duty—not our only duty, but our first duty—is to our own family and nation. Only by following this precept can we effectively give to the outsider. In national as in personal life one can give only out of strength, never out of weakness.

DOCUMENT NO. 28

CHRISTIAN CENTURY ON PEACE AIMS[*]

Charles Clayton Morrison, who edited the Christian Century *from 1908 to 1947, turned a broken-down denomination weekly into the most important Protestant journal in the world. In the* Century's *pages, Morrison promoted many social reforms, including much New Deal legislation. Though technically not a pacifist, he vigorously promoted the outlawry of war and found the Kellogg–Briand Pact of 1928 the culmination of world history to date. In a series of editorials written in 1941, he outlined his ideal world order.*

γ   γ   γ

We believe that the peace, if it is to bring a lasting surcease from war, must be negotiated in a world conference, participated in by neutral as well as belligerent states, on terms agreed upon by the belligerents. In that conference, all existing nations should share under conditions as nearly as possible approaching equality. Provision should be made for ample and free representation of the wishes of now subject peoples. It is possible that the conference might move most directly toward the accomplishment of its objectives if it divided early into two bodies, one to deal with the political and the other with the economic and social issues at stake. At the conclusion of the labors of these two bodies a plenary session of the entire conference could amalgamate the results of the negotiations by the two bodies into one peace treaty.

What might such a treaty provide? It should certainly ordain general and universal disarmament, including the disbanding of colonial armies except for necessary, but not large, police forces. In this provision would be found the answer to the objection so commonly heard as to the uselessness of negotiation with the dictators. Hitler's word might be worth no more after such a conference than it has been in the past, but Hitler without a great army would be incapable of doing the damage which he has hitherto inflicted or threatened.

Such a treaty should provide for the immediate codification of inter-

[*]"A Sketch for a Possible Peace Treaty," *Christian Century* 58 (March 12, 1941): 353–354; copyright 1941 Christian Century Foundation. Reprinted by permission from the March 12, 1941 issue of *The Christian Century*.

national law, with the principle of the outlawry of war as the corner-stone of such a new juridical structure. It should provide for a world court to administer that law, and for means whereby the law might de-velop in keeping with the changing needs of the nations.

As a workable plan for a federation of the nations, such a treaty might wisely establish regional leagues of nations. These might number five: one to be made up of the nations of the Americas, one of the nations of Europe and perhaps of those of South and North Africa, one of the na-tions of the U.S.S.R., one of the other nations of Asia, and one of the independent states of Australasia and Oceania. To these regional leagues should be committed trusteeship for all mandates. Within each regional league a customs union should be immediately established, and pledges given to develop them as rapidly as possible into autonomous economic units.

In addition, the treaty should create a world league empowered to codify international law on the recommendation of the regional leagues, to appoint members of a world court, and to establish and maintain in-ternational offices for (a) the supervision of labor standards throughout the world; (b) a continuing world economic survey; (c) a continuing world armament survey; (d) a continuing survey of the administration of mandates; (e) a continuing survey of the treatment of minorities; (f) postal, passport and Red Cross controls. A provision for the control of all armament plants by this world league might well also be included in the treaty.

The treaty should establish freedom of the seas as a fundamental principle of international law.

It should contain mutual pledges of a general reduction of tariffs to the ultimate goal of world free trade; of free markets and free access to materials in all mandates; of an end to all immigration exclusion on the basis of race; of free worship, free press, free assembly, free speech.

In the difficult field of territorial readjustments such a treaty might provide for (a) the restoration of Holland, Belgium, Denmark and Nor-way to their pre-war status; (b) an independent Poland, not necessarily with its pre-war boundaries; (c) a plebiscite to determine the disposition of Alsace and Lorraine; (d) the internationalization of all Spanish, French and Italian colonies in North Africa under a mandate system; (e) the transfer of all other African colonies to mandate status; (f) provision whereby India should join the British Commonwealth of Nations as a free republic, on the same basis as Eire; (g) confirmation of the independence of Egypt, Iran, Iraq and Syria; (h) an independent Palestine; (i) independence for Ethiopia; (j) restoration of Czechoslovakia, with a plebiscite to determine the disposition of the Sudeten area; (k) the annexation of Austria to Germany; (l) the restoration of Balkan boundaries to their pre-war status, with the exception of incorporation of the Hungarian parts of Transylvania in an independent Hungary, and the establishment of a Balkan federation; (m) the restoration to Siam of territories taken by European empires; (n) immediate independence for the Philippines; (o) the withdrawal of Japanese troops from China; (p) cancellation of all unequal treaties with China and recognition of the full sovereignty of that nation; (q) administration of Manchuria and Mongolia as mandates, with a plebiscite, say, fifteen years hence to determine their further status; (r) the transfer of French Indo-China, the Dutch East Indies and Malaysia to a mandate status; (s) provision for a plebiscite in Burma to determine whether that country should join India or maintain separate independence; (t) dismantling of all island bases in the southern Pacific, both American and Japanese.

Finally, such a treaty should provide for an American loan, to be supervised by the economic office of the new world league of nations, for the rehabilitation of Europe, China and Japan. (An alternative proposal would provide for an outright gift, making use of the gold hoard now immunized in the United States. As a means of securing a lasting peace, the cost of such a gift would be small in comparison with the costs of a war or with long-continued outlays to aid the British win a victory. In the long run, moreover, it would almost certainly prove an exceedingly profitable investment.)

DOCUMENT NO. 29

REPRESENTATIVE JOHN M. VORYS ON PEACE AIMS[*]

A member of House of Representatives from 1939 to 1959, Vorys was typical of many midwestern Republicans in opposing Roosevelt's domestic and foreign policies. He was atypical, however, in thinking in terms of a general international order.

γ   γ   γ

We learn through many leaks in the censorship that the German people want peace. Germany has had enough aerial bombing, has lost enough men, more than we lost in the entire World War, to bring the "glories" of war home to the people. Among the German people are many who fear the dynamism of Hitler, who fear that each Nazi victory merely sets the stage for further fighting, further suffering. The German soldiers in the occupied countries are becoming restless. We hear on good authority that the possible entry of America into the war brings up ominous memories in Germany. The mind readers may be wrong about Germany and peace.

Suppose, however, that Hitler will not make peace, that his offers are purely for propaganda purposes, that Hess and Funk [Walther; minister of economic affairs] and the rest are only to divide us. Then let us turn his own offers—his own tactics—against him. If we launched a peace offensive, intelligently, aggressively, and in good faith, and it failed, it would nevertheless unite our own people as they are not now united, would divide the German people, and would hearten the conquered people. The time to try it, however, is before we go in. We will never have such a chance again.

. . . .

Many Americans are struggling to formulate and state our peace aims. Their proposals are all vague and various, as they must be on a vital question that has had so little attention. They have one thing in common— none of them describes a world, an America, such as we now know.

[*]From John M. Vorys, "The Obligations of the United States as a World Power," address to Institute of Public Affairs, University of Virginia, June 24, 1941, in Appendix, *Congressional Record*, entered June 16, 1941, pp. A3100–3101.

They also reflect what every real student of this war knows—that a world revolution is going on as a part of, and cause of, and result of this war. This is violent disagreement as to just what this revolution is. It is called a revolution against the West, against Roman law, Greek logic, Christian idealism, against democracy, against the "haves," against gold and naval power. James Burnham calls it "the managerial revolution," a label approved by Stuart Chase as something different from capitalism or socialism. I can think of no better quick description than this—a revolution against traditional capitalism. It is going on in every country, going on in the United States. So far it is not our war, but it is our revolution. It is more than a wave of the future, it is the tide of the present, and the scum and guttersnipes may dirty it but they cannot control it for long. If we could only understand it, and in some way think it out instead of fighting it out, as we fought out the Protestant revolution, the French revolution, the industrial revolution, we could make this a better country, a better world. I have some suggestions for peace aims for America. Like the others, they are vague—a basis for discussion rather than a final act of demands:

First. We will preserve this country as a republic and work out the internal effects of this world-wide movement on our system by peaceful, intelligent evolution—not by violent, blind revolution.

Second. We will preserve our hemisphere intact against the military or political aggression of the world.

Third. We recognize the right of similar areas to preserve themselves intact against our military or political aggression.

Fourth. We believe that neighboring states must learn to live together peacefully in union, as we have. We will not approve of the domination of one race, or one nation, or one man. We are opposed to unions or axes based solely on color, language, race, or ideologies. We want a regime in Europe that is not a balance-of-power mosaic. We believe people who live near each other must unite in peace.

Fifth. We believe in equality of opportunity for all nations in markets, raw materials, acquiring land and emigration to all undeveloped lands.

Sixth. We believe in reciprocity of opportunity as to markets, materials, land, and emigration as between developed lands.

Seventh. We will do our part in maintaining world peace, order, and justice based on these principles. We will not enter any arrangement that inevitably involves an immediate war.

Eighth. We will participate in progressive disarmament.

DOCUMENT NO. 30

FREDA UTLEY ON NEGOTIATED PEACE[*]

The British-born Freda Utley was one of many intellectuals whose political odyssey took her from the extreme left to the extreme right. At first a Communist who worked for the Soviet trade ministry in Moscow, she became bitterly anti-Soviet after the death of her husband and ended up a fervent backer of Senator Joseph R. McCarthy. In this reading, she claimed that the United States was doing irreparable harm to Britain by encouraging it to fight a war it could not possibly win. The article first appeared in Common Sense, *a liberal monthly.*

γ   γ   γ

To those who reply to every rational argument for a negotiated peace with the phrase that "You can't trust Hitler," I say: "Granted—and a thousand times so!" Instead, we must rely upon our own strength, and upon the superiority of our own social and economic systems. A fully armed America and a reformed and rejuvenated British Empire would be strong enough to maintain the integrity of our territories and spheres of influence. If we can keep better than half the world free from Hitler we shall in the future be more than a match for a German Empire wasting its strength on the gigantic task of making slaves productive. . . .

And what peace terms can we have? Although the United States is not in a position to give victory to England, her potential influence is so enormous that by placing herself unequivocally behind Britain, but not insisting on the impossible aim of freeing the Continent of Europe by war, she could in all probability force Germany to make a peace of equals with Britain.

The common idea that the fear of America is so great in Germany that an American declaration of war would lead to an internal German collapse is, of course, fantastic; but it would seem true that the Germans are sufficiently doubtful of their ability to win a war against the United States—as distinct from their fear of losing it—as to make it

[*]From Freda Utley, "An Englishwoman Pleads: Must the World Destroy Itself?" *Reader's Digest*, October 1941, in Appendix, *Congressional Record*, entered October 23, 1941, p. 4811.

almost certain that an American offer to mediate peace on the basis of hands-off-Britain-and-her-Empire would have such an effect in Germany as to force Hitler to negotiate. . . .

There are times when there is only a choice of evils, and today the evil of accepting the fact of Nazi domination of continental Europe is less than the evil which is likely to result from encouraging England to continue indefinitely a hopeless fight until English liberties also are destroyed—either from without or from within. . . .

For what will it profit England to have held out against Hitler, and to be able to inflict upon the Germans the same sufferings she herself is enduring, if all her sacrifices cannot give her victory, and if in the meantime her trade, her productive plant, her very lifeblood have been destroyed? Wishful thinkers may reply that she will at least have preserved her freedom. But is even this sure? Is it likely that an England suffering the universal impoverishment brought about by total war would escape the fate of Germany after the last war? It is hard to see how our liberal and humanitarian values can survive the aftermath of a long and increasingly bitter war. . . .

Out of universal war on the total scale no good can come, only perhaps an even worse, or a more universal, evil than Hitlerism. But there is at least some hope that, with peace, the foundations of Hitler's tyranny may be destroyed. The German people are of the same flesh and blood as ourselves and must yearn for something else in life besides sacrifices and death, bloody glory, and the hatred of their neighbors. The universal testimony is that the older Nazi soldiers—the married men—in the occupied countries are restless and want peace. German morale, which alone can preserve the German Reich, will not endure if Hitler's promise of a peaceful, prosperous, and better-ordered world fails to materialize.

It is possible to hope that after her victories have wiped out the memory of past defeats, national humiliation, and the material privations of the past quarter of a century, and once she has no cause to envy the great territorial possessions of Britain and France, Germany may rid herself of the gangsters who now rule her, and revert to the civilized values which alone can give a people permanent satisfaction. The prospect is less hopeless than continuation of the war until there is universal wretchedness and despair.

While the disarmed millions in the occupied countries cannot revolt, the German people may find means of changing their government.

There is the reasonable hope that her leaders, bloody-minded men, may divide. In war the Nazis go from strength to strength, for their power is founded upon the emotions which war breeds. Peace might give a chance to other elements in Germany to assert themselves. The army may transfer its allegiance to new leaders when peace shall have brought the Germans to think as citizens rather than as soldiers. This happened in both Germany and Russia after the last war.

Perhaps it is an unconscious realization of all these real factors which is keeping the American people from participation in the war as belligerents. The last war having resulted in the destruction of democracy over all Europe east of the Rhine, there is now an underlying distrust among Americans as to the possibility of saving democracy by once again sacrificing millions of young men in Europe's wars. The idea was well expressed by the late Lord Lothian [British ambassador to U.S.]: "The lesson of the last war is that we get neither democracy, nor liberty, nor peace out of a world war, however noble the end for which it is fought."

DOCUMENT NO. 31

ROBERT M. HUTCHINS ON
DOMESTIC PRIORITIES*

An outstanding academician and later a foundation executive, Hutchins was deemed "the boy wonder" of higher education. President of the University of Chicago at age thirty, he gained a national reputation for his innovative educational philosophy. A strong reformer, he represented that wing of anti-interventionism that feared war would terminate social improvement in the United States.

γ   γ   γ

If we stay out of war, we may perhaps some day understand and practice freedom of speech, freedom of worship, freedom from want, and freedom from fear. We may even be able to comprehend and support justice, democracy, the moral order, and the supremacy of human rights. Today we have barely begun to grasp the meaning of the words. . . .

Have we freedom of speech and freedom of worship in this country? We do have freedom to say what everybody else is saying and freedom of worship if we do not take our religion too seriously. But teachers who do not conform to the established canons of social thought lose their jobs. People who are called radicals have mysterious difficulties in renting halls. Labor organizers sometimes get beaten up and ridden out of town on a rail. Norman Thomas had some troubles in Jersey City. And the Daughters of the American Revolution refused to let Marian Anderson sing in the National Capital in a building called Constitution Hall.

If we regard these exceptions as minor, reflecting the attitude of the more backward and illiterate parts of the country, what are we to say of freedom from want and freedom from fear? What of the moral order and justice and the supremacy of human rights? What of democracy in the United States?

Words like these have no meaning unless we believe in human dignity. Human dignity means that every man is an end in himself. No man can be exploited by another. Think of these things and then think

*From Robert M. Hutchins, "America and the War," radio address of January 23, 1941, in Appendix, *Congressional Record*, entered January 29, 1941, pp. A303–304.

of the sharecroppers, the "okies," the Negroes, the slum dwellers, downtrodden and oppressed for gain. They have neither freedom from want nor freedom from fear. They hardly know they are living in a moral order or in a democracy where justice and human rights are supreme.

We have it on the highest authority that one-third of the Nation is ill-fed, ill-clothed, and ill-housed. The latest figures of the National Resources Board show that almost precisely 55 percent of our people are living on family incomes of less than $1,250 a year. This sum, says Fortune magazine, will not support a family of four. On this basis more than half our people are living below the minimum level of subsistence. More than half the army which will defend democracy will be drawn from those who have had this experience of the economic benefits of the American way of life. . . .

As for democracy, we know that millions of men and women are disfranchised in this country because of their race, color, or condition of economic servitude. We know that many municipal governments are models of corruption. Some State governments are merely the shadows of big-city machines. Our national Government is a Government by pressure groups. Almost the last question an American is expected to ask about a proposal is whether it is just. The question is how much pressure is there behind it or how strong are the interests against it. On this basis are settled such great issues as monopoly, the organization of agriculture, the relation of labor and capital, whether bonuses should be paid to veterans, and whether a tariff policy based on greed should be modified by reciprocal trade agreements. . . .

In the speech in which Mr. Roosevelt told us, in effect, that we are headed for war, he said, "Certainly, this is no time to stop thinking about the social and economic problems which are the root cause of the social revolution which is today a supreme factor in the world." But in the same speech he said, "The need of the moment is that our actions and our policy should be devoted primarily—almost exclusively—to meeting this foreign peril. For all our domestic problems are now a part of the great emergency." This means—and it is perfectly obvious—that if any social objective interferes with the conduct of the war, it will be, it must be, instantly abandoned. War can mean only the loss of social gains and the destruction of the livelihood of millions in modest circumstances, while pirates and profiteers, in spite of Mr. Roosevelt's efforts to stop them, emerge stronger than ever.

DOCUMENT NO. 32

WILLIAM R. CASTLE ON
ACCOMMODATION WITH JAPAN*

A career diplomat, Castle served as assistant secretary of state (1927–1929), ambassador to Japan (1929–1931), and undersecretary of state (1931). Castle was a strong conservative who opposed the New Deal on constitutional and monetary grounds. During his career he always sought U.S. accommodation with Japan, which—he believed—would moderate aggressive tendencies.

γ   γ   γ

TO THE NEW YORK HERALD TRIBUNE:

Everything points in these days to the possibility, not to say probability, of war with Japan. People like our bellicose Secretary of the Navy announce that trouble is inevitable, and this goes a long way toward making trouble inevitable by stirring up the Japanese. Along with this talk of probable war, however, one repeatedly hears the question, "Why should we go to war with Japan?" To that question I have never received a reasonable answer, except the answer always made by those who feel we should interfere anywhere in the world on the side of a nation unjustly attacked.

These people say that we must fight Japan because Japan unjustly attacked China. This is an understandable answer and one must respect the people who honestly make it, although it is appallingly bad reasoning. It is clear, however, that war between the United States and Japan, however it came out, would be an unhappy thing for both countries. It might be a long war, exhausting to both. It might be a disastrous war, helping to destroy the economic standards and ability of both countries. There is no possible doubt that, with our superior resources, we should win in the end, but we cannot sink the Japanese islands, although we might be able to burn Tokio; and we should create, in place of a friendly nation which is one of our best customers, a sullen and revengeful nation.

*William R. Castle, letter to editor, *New York Herald Tribune*, December 7, 1941.

I was publicly debating the subject with one of the most vigorous proponents of "all out" aid to China, which, as it is interpreted by most people, means war with Japan. He admitted in his opening statement that the Japanese must have access to raw materials and therefore must expand politically in order to assure economic access to neighboring markets. In rebuttal I quite naturally asked him where he would expect Japan to expand. He answered that almost anywhere would do so long as it left China alone, and when pressed to be specific he did not see why Japan should not take over Indo-China. And yet it is a fact that the Japanese occupation of certain areas in Indo-China, with the consent of the government of Vichy—a consent very probably obtained at the muzzle of a gun—has, more than anything else, turned the United States against Japan. It is true that we have no great interests in Indo-China, but it is also true that we fear Indo-China would be used as a stepping stone to the East Indies.

We fear also that the control of Indo-China is a threat against Singapore, and we are apparently just about as ready to go to war to insure the safety of different parts of the British Empire as we are to insure our own safety. Would it not be more reasonable for us to oppose Japan's overlordship of Indo-China on the ground that it threatens Malaya, on which we are far more dependent for rubber than we are on the Dutch East Indies? This occupation constitutes no particular threat to the Philippines, which are, in any case, open to attack direct from Japan.

It is said that if we seek to renew cordial relations with Japan we shall be destroying China. There is little in this statement. In renewing trade with Japan we should not promise to stop our trade with China. The Japanese would not expect to cut relations with China, because, under no circumstances at present foreseeable, should we become an ally of Japan! The outcry about our furnishing Japan with the sinews of war against China has always been exaggerated. Only a small part of the oil and the cotton we have sent to Japan has been used in the war against China. Japan is a great industrial nation which consumes these things itself. There is also an immense peacetime trade with Japan which helps both nations.

Furthermore, the very fact of our opening our markets to Japan would minimize the danger of Japanese attack on the Dutch East Indies. Any industrial nation must have oil, and if we do not only refuse to sell oil, but urge the government of the Indies to refuse to sell, the outcome, deplorable as it would be, would seem almost inevitable. President Roosevelt explained that we had sold oil to Japan for this very reason—and the reason is as valid today as a year ago.

It is also said that the administration refuses to discuss the matter of improving relations with Japan until Japan gets out of China. It would seem that almost any intelligent man would see the futility of such a demand. You cannot ask a nation at war to surrender because it would mean, probably, complete collapse and revolution at home. The four hundred millions of China will never be defeated permanently by the eighty millions of Japan. And for the long future of the Orient, it is better that Japan learn this lesson now. . . .

There is another reason why war with Japan at this particular time would be exceedingly unwise, not to say disastrous. We are exerting every effort, in my opinion rightly, to send war supplies of all kinds to England in the heroic fight Britain is making against Nazi Germany. If we should go to war with Japan the inevitable consequence of such a move would be, first, that we should have to keep the major portion of our fleet in the Pacific, and second, that we should have to cut drastically our exports of war materials to England. The people of America, especially those of the Pacific Coast, would certainly insist that, as we were at war in the Pacific, we must hold onto our airplanes and our big guns for our own use. The political force of that appeal would be almost irresistible and Britain would be sadly crippled. I was discussing this matter, shortly before his death, with Lord Lothian, who said he was afraid he had to agree that war between America and Japan would be a prime disaster for Britain.

Among many others there is one more reason against war with Japan which appeals to me more than any other; that is that the man who wants such a war more than any other individual is Adolf Hitler. It is absurd to know what Hitler is thinking, but in this case we have proof from the fact that his agents in Japan are inciting the Japanese to take actions which may cause trouble with the United States. The Germans long for such a war for reasons which must be obvious to every one. Are we then going to be so foolish as to play directly into Hitler's hands? Why do we not remember that first things come first?

> W. R. CASTLE
> Washington, D.C., Dec. 1, 1941.

DOCUMENT 33

NEW YORK DAILY NEWS
ON A TWO-FRONT WAR*

The New York Daily News *was published by Joseph M. Patterson, under whose direction it had the largest daily circulation in the United States. Unlike many anti-interventionists, the* News *strongly defended the New Deal. In 1940 its editorials endorsing a third term for Roosevelt helped win it a Pulitzer Prize. The* News *had sought to embargo Japan until June 1940, when it claimed that only accommodation would prevent the United States from facing enemies in both Europe and Asia.*

γ   γ   γ

FIGHT GERMANY AND JAPAN

Secretary of the Navy Frank Knox has two or three times vetoed the general Washington feeling that a United States–Japan war is just around the corner. As levelheaded and realistic an observer as Gen. Hugh S. Johnson remarked sadly last week that he considered war with Japan inevitable.

The question that keeps stumping us is: Why? Why, especially when we are already at war by sea and moving as rapidly as the President can drag us toward all-out war with one of the most successful and ruthless conquerors of all time?

If the United States had any real quarrel with Japan, or if Japan were showing signs of sending ships or planes, or both, to hammer our western fortress of Hawaii, our west coast cities, and our San Pedro naval base we'd say sure, let's take them on, no matter what other wars we're engaged in. We'd have to take them on, and give them the best fight we could.

But Japan is badly tangled up with the Chinese, to begin with, and has to keep large forces on its Russian frontier with Manchukuo. What Japan wants is more of China, probably all of French Indochina, some of Siam, and at least a free commercial hand in the East Indies.

We keep telling Japan that it can have none of these things; that our

*"Fight Germany and Japan?" *New York Daily News*, November 17, 1941, p. 23 in Appendix, *Congressional Record*, November 17, 1941, p. A5152.

dignity or ideals or whatnot will be outraged, and we'll have to fight if it goes any farther. Why?

Of all the oriental peoples, the Japanese are the most nearly like us.

OCCIDENTAL ORIENTALS

They are fond of machinery, and are good at making and operating airplanes, automobiles, steamships. They like gadgets of all kinds, as do we. They are trade-minded and acquisitive. They are physically clean. They even, alone among oriental peoples, think baseball is a fine game, and like both to play it and to watch it.

The Japanese are fiercely patriotic, whereas most other orientals are not, because of centuries of oppression by war lords, sultans, maharajahs, etc. And let us make no mistake about it, the Japs are excellent fighters. Their islands have never been invaded in recorded history. The Mongol Emperor Kublai Khan, conqueror of everything else he tackled, was the last man to try to invade Japan to date. Kublai's ears were pinned back by the Japanese in 1274, and again in 1281. He was planning a third try when he died in 1294, but his successors thought better of it.

A WAR ON TWO FRONTS

We are giving up our major territorial interest in the far Pacific. Legislation cutting the Philippines loose in 1946 is on our books, legislation which the Filipinos, who always have disliked us, kept begging us to enact. The Filipinos have lately taken most of the independence talk back, true; but the intent of that law is that we are getting out of our Far East misadventure.

Most Americans, we are convinced, don't want to fight Japan. Especially does no sensible American want a two-front war, against Germany to the east and Japan to the west, at the same time.

The only answer that we can figure out to this "inevitable" war with Japan is that our administration feels obligated to shore up the British Empire in the Far East.

We are already helping the British keep their island home off the European mainland; and the nation we are helping them fend off is the world's most formidable land power at this time. Isn't that enough? Or must we become out-and-out vassals of the British Empire, to do its bidding all around the world for all time so far ahead as we can see?

DOCUMENT NO. 34

CHRISTIAN CENTURY ON
U.S. PEACE TERMS WITH JAPAN[*]

Even three weeks prior to the outbreak of war, the nation's leading Protestant journal took advantage of the arrival of Japan's special envoy, Saburo Kurusu, to indicate that peace was still possible. As part of its peace terms, said the Christian Century, *the United States must accord Japan equality of racial status and equal access to raw materials.*

γ　　　　　　　γ　　　　　　　γ

It is no secret that the whole colonial structure of the white empires is threatening to fall apart unless we intervene in Asia. Many British leaders would welcome American involvement with Japan. This is especially true because the Axis alliance against America, by which Japan was attached to Germany and Italy, automatically insures that our participation in Asiatic wars will also involve us in the European struggle. So the thesis of Sidney Rogerson's pre-war book, *Propaganda in the Next War*—that the surest way Britain can bring the United States to her aid will be to involve us in war with Japan—is being validated by events.

The immediate issue in the present situation is oil. Japan produces only about one-tenth of her requirements in the territories under her control. Her troops in Indo-China are in a position to threaten oil supplies in the Netherlands Indies and in British Burma. The latter field is probably easier of access and might therefore be the first object of attack. Hence Mr. Churchill's concern as to Japan's next move. Since an attack in this direction would, if successful, also cut the Burma road, the only remaining route through which supplies from the United States can now reach Chungking, there is double reason to believe it may be made. The blunt warning which the Japanese embassy in Washington issued recently, declaring that Japan could not survive without oil and would soon take steps to get it, peacefully if possible, but otherwise if not, indicates where the present tension has its source. And the

[*]From "One Chance in Ten," *Christian Century* 58 (November 19, 1941): 1432–1434; copyright 1941 Christian Century Foundation. Reprinted by permission from the November 19, 1941 issue of *The Christian Century*.

extraordinary meeting of the Japanese Diet on November 15 indicates that the decision may come soon.

The negotiators who are about to face each other in Washington are therefore confronted by alternatives which cannot be resolved peacefully unless one side or the other—or both—back down. President Roosevelt has declared that it would be intolerable for this country to live being "fed through the bars" raised by the Axis powers, yet this is exactly the situation which this country, aided doubtfully by the Netherlands and Britain, imposes upon Japan. The conditions on which the United States is willing to lift the bars are understood to be Japanese evacuation of China, Indo-China and renunciation of the Axis alliance. So far as is known, no guarantees have been given that if she complies, Japan will be accorded equality of racial status or equal security of access to raw materials now so largely controlled by the British, Dutch and ourselves. Her leaders may well assume that if she complies, she will simply be classified as "unfinished business" to be quieted now and summarily disposed of when the more pressing claims of Europe are satisfied. While there can be no excuse for the policy Japan has followed in recent years or disposition to minimize the fact that the present dangerous impasse is the logical fruit of her perverse and bellicose leadership, it should not be hard to understand why the Tokyo cabinet might prefer the perils of war now to the prospects of such a future.

The United States alone retains its full freedom of action in the situation. We alone are not irrevocably committed—at least so far as the public knows. While it is inconceivable that any American would support a policy which would betray China into the hands of her oppressor, this nation can afford to be considerate and generous with Japan. The war-weary Japanese people would overnight reject any government which would refuse to accept an assurance from the United States that the island empire would be accorded full equality in treatment at a post-war conference. But the eighth point of the Atlantic Charter stands in the way of that. It warns the Japanese that if Mr. Roosevelt and Mr. Churchill determine the shape of the post-war world, the Axis powers will be disarmed while the victors retain their guns. Japan will never consent to servile acceptance of a destiny meted out to her on these terms.

America is not committed to the Atlantic Charter. It has never been accepted by the United States Senate, which alone under the Constitution can commit this nation by approving treaties. Japan is said to be

willing to renounce her Axis ties if this country will recognize Manchukuo. That, as a temporary expedient, is at least a subject for negotiation. Japan will have to remove her army from China and to hold her
occupation of Indo-China subject to the post-war settlement. A public
declaration by our government of its intention to treat Japan as an equal
in the post-war peace conference would dispose of the Atlantic Charter.
War can be avoided.

Ambassador Kurusu describes his chances of reaching a solution in
Washington as about one in ten. That is probably an optimistic estimate. But it shows that the die is not yet cast. If there is a will to peace
in Washington, war is not inevitable. A desire to treat Japan as we would
ask to be treated, based on recognition that all the sins have not been
committed on one side, will make that one chance in ten adequate for
peace.

BIBLIOGRAPHY

PRIMARY SOURCES

Baldwin, Hanson W. *United We Stand!: Defense of Western Hemisphere* (New York: Whittlesey House, 1941).

Baxter, William J. *America and Japan Must Work Together* (New York: International Economic Research Bureau, 1940).

Beals, Carleton. *Pan America: A Program for the Western Hemisphere* (Boston: Houghton Mifflin, 1940).

Beard, Charles A. *A Foreign Policy for America* (New York: Knopf, 1940).

Beard, Charles A. *Giddy Minds and Foreign Quarrels: An Estimate of American Foreign Policy* (New York: Macmillan, 1939).

Borchard, Edwin and Lage, William Potter. *Neutrality for the United States* (New Haven: Yale University Press, rev. ed. 1940).

Carter, Boake. *Why Meddle in Europe? Facts, Figures, Fictions and Follies* (New York: Robert M. McBride, 1939).

Chamberlain, John. *The American Stakes* (Philadelphia: Lippincott, 1940).

Chase, Stuart with Tyler, Marian. *The New Western Front* (New York: Harcourt Brace, 1939).

Dennis, Lawrence. *The Dynamics of War and Revolution* (New York: Weekly Foreign Letter, 1940).

Doenecke, Justus D., ed. *In Danger Undaunted: The Anti-Interventionist Movement of 1940–1941 as Revealed in the Papers of the America First Committee* (Stanford, Calif.: Hoover Institution Press, 1990).

Flynn, John T. *Country Squire in the White House* (New York: Doubleday, Doran, 1940).

Grattan, C. Hartley. *The Deadly Parallel* (New York: Stackpole, 1939).

Gronowicz, Anthony, ed. *Oswald Garrison Villard: The Dilemmas of the Absolute Pacifist in Two World Wars* (New York: Garland, 1983).

Howard, Graeme K. *America and a New World Order* (New York: Scribner's, 1940).

Johnpoll, Bernard F., ed. *Norman Thomas on War: An Anthology* (New York: Garland, 1974).

Johnson, Hugh S. *Hell-Bent for War* (Indianapolis: Bobbs-Merrill, 1941).

Lindbergh, Anne Morrow. *War Within and Without: Diaries and Letters, 1939–1944* (New York: Harcourt Brace Jovanovich, 1980).

Lindbergh, Anne Morrow. *The Wave of the Future: A Confession of Faith* (New York: Harcourt Brace, 1940).

Lindbergh, Charles A. *The Wartime Journals of Charles A. Lindbergh* (New York: Harcourt Brace Jovanovich, 1970).

MacLiesh, Fleming and Reynolds, Cushman. *Strategy of the Americas* (New York: Duell, Sloan and Pearce, 1941).

Muste, A. J. *Non-Violence in an Aggressive World* (New York: Harper, 1941).

Nixon, Larry, ed. *What Will Happen and What to Do When War Comes* (New York: Greystone, 1939).

Sargent, Porter. *Getting Us into War* (Boston: Porter Sargent, 1941).

Schoonmaker, Nancy and Reid, Doris Fielding, eds. *We Testify* (New York: Smith and Durrell, 1941).

Thomas, Norman. *We Have a Future* (Princeton, N.J.: Princeton University Press, 1940).

Thomas, Norman and Wolfe, Bertram D. *Keep America Out of War: A Program.* (New York: Frederick A. Stokes, 1939).

Utley, Freda. *The Dream We Lost: Soviet Russia Then and Now.* (New York: John Day, 1940).

Villard, Oswald Garrison. *Our Military Chaos: The Truth About Defense* (New York: Knopf, 1939).

Williams, Al. *Airpower* (New York: Coward-McCann, 1940).

MEMOIRS

Fish, Hamilton. *Memoir of an American Patriot* (Washington, D.C.: Regnery Gateway, 1991).

Libby, Frederick J. *To End War: The Story of the National Council for the Prevention of War* (Nyack, N.Y.: Fellowship Publications, 1969).

Lindbergh, Charles A. *Autobiography of Values* (New York: Harcourt Brace Jovanovich, 1978).

Utley, Freda. *Odyssey of a Liberal: Memoirs.* (Washington, D.C.: Washington National Press, 1970).

Wheeler, Burton K. with Healy, Paul F. *Yankee from the West* (Garden City, N.Y.: Doubleday, 1962).

SECONDARY SOURCES

Bailey, Thomas A. and Ryan, Paul B. *Hitler vs. Roosevelt: The Undeclared Naval War* (New York: Free Press, 1979).

Beard, Charles A. *American Foreign Policy in the Making, 1932–1940: A Study in Responsibilities* (New Haven: Yale University Press, 1946).

Beard, Charles A. *President Roosevelt and the Coming of the War, 1941: A Study in Appearances and Realities* (New Haven: Yale University Press, 1948).

Beschloss, Michael D. *Kennedy and Roosevelt: The Uneasy Alliance* (New York: Norton, 1980).

Best, Gary Dean. *Herbert Hoover: The Postpresidential Years, 1933–1964*, 2 vols. (Stanford, Calif.: Hoover Institution Press, 1983).

Cantril, Hadley and Strunk, Mildred, eds. *Public Opinion, 1935—1946* (Princeton, N.J.: Princeton University Press, 1951).

Carlisle, Rodney. "The Foreign Policy Views of an Isolationist Press Lord: W. R. Hearst and the International Crisis, 1936–1941," *Journal of Contemporary History* 9 (July 1974): 217–227.

Chadwin, Mark Lincoln. *The Hawks of World War II* (Chapel Hill: University of North Carolina Press, 1968).

Chatfield, Charles. *For Peace and Justice: Pacifism in America, 1914–1941* (Knoxville: University of Tennessee Press, 1971).

Clifford, J. Garry and Spencer, Samuel R., Jr., *The First Peacetime Draft* (Lawrence: University of Kansas Press, 1986).

Cole, Wayne S. "The America First Committee: What Might Have Been," *Chronicles: A Magazine of American Culture* 15 (December 1991): 20–22.

Cole, Wayne S. *America First: The Battle Against Intervention, 1940–1941* (Madison: University of Wisconsin Press, 1953).

Cole, Wayne S. *Charles A. Lindbergh and the Battle Against American Intervention in World War II* (New York: Harcourt Brace Jovanovich, 1974).

Cole, Wayne S. *Roosevelt and the Isolationists, 1932–45* (Lincoln: University of Nebraska Press, 1983).

Cole, Wayne S. *Senator Gerald P. Nye and American Foreign Relations* (Minneapolis: University of Minnesota, 1962).

Compton, James V. *The Swastika and the Eagle: Hitler, the United States, and the Origins of World War II* (Boston: Houghton Mifflin, 1967).

Cull, Nicholas John. *Selling War: The British Propaganda Campaign Against American "Neutrality" in World War II* (New York: Oxford University Press, 1995).

Dallek, Robert. *Franklin D. Roosevelt and American Foreign Policy, 1932–1945* (New York: Oxford University Press, 1979).

Dawson, Raymond H. *The Decision to Aid Russia, 1941: Foreign Policy and Domestic Politics* (Chapel Hill: University of North Carolina Press, 1959).

Diamond, Sander A. *The Nazi Movement in the United States, 1924–1941* (Ithaca, N.Y.: Cornell University Press, 1974).

Divine, Robert A. *Foreign Policy and U.S. Presidential Elections, 1940–1960.* 2 vols. (New York: New Viewpoints, 1974).

Doenecke, Justus D. *Anti-Intervention: A Bibliographical Introduction to Isolationism and Pacifism from World War I to the Early Cold War* (New York: Garland, 1987).

Doenecke, Justus D. "The Isolationism of Robert E. Wood," in John N. Schacht, ed. *Three Faces of Midwestern Isolationism* (Iowa City, Iowa: Center for the Study of the Recent History of the United States, 1981), pp. 11–22.

Doenecke, Justus D. "Germany in Isolationist Ideology, 1939–1941: The Issue of a Negotiated Peace," in Hans L. Trefousse, ed., *Germany and America:*

Essays on Problems of International Relations and Immigration (New York: Brooklyn College Press, 1980), pp. 215–226.

Doenecke, Justus D. "Historiography: U.S. Policy and the European War, 1939–1941," *Diplomatic History* 19 (Fall 1995): 669–698.

Doenecke, Justus D. "Isolationism of the Left: The Keep America Out of War Congress, 1938–1941," *Journal of Contemporary History* 12 (April 1977): 221–236.

Doenecke, Justus D. "The Isolationist as Collectivist: Lawrence Dennis and the Coming of World War II," *Journal of Libertarian Studies* 3 (Summer 1979): 191–207.

Doenecke, Justus D. "Rehearsal for Cold War: United States Anti-Interventionists and the Soviet Union, 1939–1941," *International Journal of Politics, Culture and Society* 7 (Spring 1994): 375–392.

Doenecke, Justus D. and Wilz, John E. *From Isolation to War, 1931–1941* (2nd ed.; Arlington Heights, Ill.: Harlan Davidson, 1991).

Edwards, Jerome E. *The Foreign Policy of Col. McCormick's Tribune, 1929–1941* (Reno: University of Nevada Press, 1971).

Foster, Carrie A. *The Women and the Warriors: The U.S. Section of the Women's International League for Peace and Freedom, 1915–1946* (Syracuse: Syracuse University Press, 1995).

Friedländer, Saul. *Prelude to Downfall: Hitler and the United States, 1939–1941* (New York: Knopf, 1967).

Frye, Alton. *Nazi Germany and the American Hemisphere, 1933–1941* (New Haven: Yale University Press, 1967).

Gallup, George H. *The Gallup Poll: Public Opinion, 1935–1971*, 3 vols. (Westport, Conn.: Greenwood, 1977).

Gellman, Irwin F. *Secret Affairs: Franklin Roosevelt, Cordell Hull and Sumner Welles* (Baltimore: Johns Hopkins University Press, 1995).

Goddard, Arthur, ed. *Harry Elmer Barnes, Learned Crusader: The New History in Action* (Colorado Springs, Colo.: Ralph Myles, 1968).

Guinsburg, Thomas N. *The Pursuit of Isolationism in the United States Senate from Versailles to Pearl Harbor* (New York: Garland, 1982).

Haines, Gerald K. "Roads to War: United States Foreign Policy, 1931–1941," in G. K. Haines and J. Samuel Walker, eds. *American Foreign Relations: A Historiographical Survey* (Westport, Conn.: Greenwood, 1981), pp. 159–185.

Heinrichs, Waldo. *Threshold of War: Franklin D. Roosevelt and American Entry into World War II* (New York: Oxford University Press, 1988).

Howlett, Charles F. *The American Peace Movement: References and Resources* (Boston: G. K. Hall, 1991).

Iriye, Akira. *The Origins of the Second World War in Asia and the Pacific* (New York: Longman, 1987).

Jacobs, Travis Beal. *America and the Winter War, 1939–1940* (New York: Garland, 1981).

Johnpoll, Bernard K. *Pacifist's Progress: Norman Thomas and the Decline of American Socialism* (Chicago: Quadrangle, 1970).

Johnson, Walter. *The Battle Against Isolation* (Chicago: University of Chicago Press, 1944).

Jonas, Manfred. *Isolationism in America, 1935–1941* (Ithaca, N.Y.: Cornell University Press, 1966).

Jonas, Manfred. "Pro-Axis Sentiment and American Isolationism," *Historian* 29 (February 1967): 221–237.

Kimball, Warren F. *The Most Unsordid Act: Lend-Lease, 1939–1941* (Baltimore: Johns Hopkins Press, 1969).

Langer, William L. and Gleason, S. Everett. *The Challenge to Isolation, 1937–1940* (New York: Harper, 1952).

Langer, William L. and Gleason, S. Everett. *The Undeclared War, 1940–1941* (New York: Harper, 1953).

Leigh, Michael. *Mobilizing Consent: Public Opinion and American Foreign Policy, 1937–1947* (Westport, Conn.: Greenwood, 1976).

Lower, Richard Coke. *A Bloc of One: The Political Career of Hiram W. Johnson* (Stanford, Calif.: Stanford University Press, 1993).

MacDonnell, Francis. *Insidious Foes: The Axis Fifth Column and the American Home Front* (New York: Oxford University Press, 1995).

Maddox, Robert James. *William E. Borah and American Foreign Policy* (Baton Rouge: Louisiana State University Press, 1969).

Maney, Patrick J. *"Young Bob" La Follette: A Biography of Robert M. La Follette, Jr., 1895–1953* (Columbia: University of Missouri Press, 1978).

Marcus, Sheldon. *Father Coughlin: The Tumultuous Life of the Priest of the Little Flower* (Boston: Little Brown, 1973).

McKenna, Marian C. *Borah* (Ann Arbor: University of Michigan Press, 1961).

Meyer, Donald B. *The Protestant Search for Political Realism, 1919–1941* (Berkeley: University of California Press, 1960).

Muresianu, John M. *War of Ideas: American Intellectuals and the World Crisis, 1938–1945* (New York: Garland, 1988).

Nore, Ellen. *Charles A. Beard: A Biography* (Carbondale: Southern Illinois University Press, 1983).

O'Reilly, Kenneth. "A New Deal for the FBI: The Roosevelt Administration, Crime Control, and National Security," *Journal of American History* 69 (December 1982): 638–658.

Patterson, James T. *Mr. Republican: A Biography of Robert A. Taft* (Boston: Houghton Mifflin, 1972).

Porter, David L. *The Seventy-sixth Congress and World War II, 1939–1940* (Columbia: University of Missouri Press, 1979).

Radosh, Ronald. *Prophets on the Right: Profiles of Conservative Critics of American Globalism* (New York: Simon and Schuster, 1975).

Reynolds, David. *The Creation of the Anglo-American Alliance, 1937-1941: A Study of Competitive Co-operation* (Chapel Hill: University of North Carolina, 1981).

Robinson, Joann Ooiman, *Abraham Went Out: A Biography of A. J. Muste* (Philadelphia: Temple University Press, 1981).

Russett, Bruce M. *No Clear and Present Danger: A Skeptical View of the U.S. Entry into World War II* (New York: Harper Torchbooks, 1972).

Schneider, James C. *Should America Go to War? The Debate over Foreign Policy in Chicago, 1939-1941* (Chapel Hill: University of North Carolina Press, 1989).

Smith, Geoffrey S. "Isolationism, the Devil, and the Advent of World War II: Variations on the Theme," *International History Review* 4 (February 1982): 55-89.

Smith, Geoffrey S. *To Save a Nation: American Countersubversives, the New Deal, and the Coming of the New Deal* (New York: Basic, 1973).

Steele, Richard W. "Franklin D. Roosevelt and His Foreign Policy Critics," *Political Science Quarterly* 94 (Spring 1979): 15-32.

Stenehjem, Michele Flynn. *An American First: John T. Flynn and the America First Committee* (New Rochelle, N.Y.: Arlington House, 1976).

Swanberg, W. A. *Norman Thomas: The Last Idealist* (New York: Scribner's 1976).

Tompkins, C. David. *Senator Arthur H. Vandenberg: The Evolution of a Modern Republican, 1884-1945* (East Lansing: Michigan State University Press, 1970).

Trefousse, Hans L. *Germany and American Neutrality, 1939-1941* (New York: Bookman, 1951).

Trefousse, Hans L. *Pearl Harbor: The Continuing Controversy* (Malabar, Fla.: Krieger, 1982).

Weinberg, Gerhard L. *A World at Arms: A Global History of World War II* (New York: Cambridge University Press, 1994).

Weinberg, Gerhard L. *World in the Balance: Behind the Scenes of World War II* (Hanover, N. H.: Brandeis University Press, 1981).

Wilson, Theodore A. *The First Summit: Roosevelt and Churchill at Placentia Bay 1941* (rev. ed.; Lawrence: University of Kansas, 1991).

Wreszin, Michael. *Oswald Garrison Villard: Pacifist at War* (Bloomington: Indiana University Press, 1965).

INDEX